THE MACRON RÉGIME
The Ideology of the New Right in France

Charles Devellennes

First published in Great Britain in 2024 by

Bristol University Press
University of Bristol
1-9 Old Park Hill
Bristol
BS2 8BB
UK
t: +44 (0)117 374 6645
e: bup-info@bristol.ac.uk

Details of international sales and distribution partners are available at bristoluniversitypress.co.uk

© Bristol University Press 2024

British Library Cataloguing in Publication Data
A catalogue record for this book is available from the British Library

ISBN 978-1-5292-2708-6 hardcover
ISBN 978-1-5292-2709-3 paperback
ISBN 978-1-5292-2710-9 ePub
ISBN 978-1-5292-2711-6 ePdf

The right of Charles Devellennes to be identified as author of this work has been asserted by him in accordance with the Copyright, Designs and Patents Act 1988.

All rights reserved: no part of this publication may be reproduced, stored in a retrieval system, or transmitted in any form or by any means, electronic, mechanical, photocopying, recording, or otherwise without the prior permission of Bristol University Press.

Every reasonable effort has been made to obtain permission to reproduce copyrighted material. If, however, anyone knows of an oversight, please contact the publisher.

The statements and opinions contained within this publication are solely those of the author and not of the University of Bristol or Bristol University Press. The University of Bristol and Bristol University Press disclaim responsibility for any injury to persons or property resulting from any material published in this publication.

Bristol University Press works to counter discrimination on grounds of gender, race, disability, age and sexuality.

Cover design: Liam Roberts Design
Front cover image: Shutterstock/vector_brothers

Contents

List of Abbreviations		iv
Acknowledgements		v
Introduction		1
1	A New Régime	17
2	Security	39
3	Merit	60
4	Hope	77
Conclusion		96
References		113
Index		121

List of Abbreviations

EELV	Europe Écologie Les Verts
EMS	European Monetary System
ENA	École Nationale d'Administration
ENS	École Normale Supérieure
EU	European Union
FN	Front National
GDP	gross domestic product
IFI	Impôt sur la Fortune Immobilière
IMF	International Monetary Fund
Insee	Institut national de la statistique et des études économiques
ISF	Impôt de Solidarité sur la Fortune
LFI	La France Insoumize
LR	Les Républicains
LREM	La République en Marche
MoDem	Mouvement Démocrate
PCF	Parti Communiste Français
PM	prime minister
PS	Parti Socialiste
RN	Rassemblement National
SNCF	Société Nationale des Chemins de Fer Français
VGE	Valéry Giscard d'Estaing

Acknowledgements

This book could not have happened in the relatively short space of time it took to write without considerable support from those around me, and without the countless conversations about French politics I inflicted upon them. After the *gilets jaunes* took to the streets in late 2018, it appeared pressing to show the Macron régime's political colours, which were very much to the right but not conservative. Many reflections came to the fore of those debates we had had during the classes I taught on conservative political thought, and I am thankful to my students for having pushed my thinking on these issues. I also largely benefited from discussions on political theory over the past decades, which have shaped my thinking around the political situation in France. Specifically, I would like to thank those who have contributed to the present volume in recent discussions, particularly Timothy Aistrope, Nicolas Baygert, Yana Bezirganova, Alexandre Christoyannopoulos, Susan Collard, Philip Cunliffe, Henry and Hugo Deslongchamps, Yves and Fabienne Devellennes, Fanny Forest, George Hoare, Alex Hochuli, Morvan Lallouet, Tadeusz Markiewicz, James Martel, Edward Martin, Edward Morgan-Jones, Aino Petterson and Robert Wilson. Finally, I would like to thank the staff at Bristol University Press, notably Stephen Wenham for his very helpful comments on all drafts, and Zoë Forbes for getting the book over the line, as well as the anonymous reviewers whose comments helped me improve the book.

Introduction

Liberté, égalité, fraternité is the motto of the French Republic. From revolutionary times to today, liberty, equality and fraternity have resonated as core values of all types of republicans, from left to right, and act as a profession of faith highlighting common values, aspirations and beliefs. The three values have survived changes in political régimes, the erosion of the centuries, wars, counter-revolutions and civil strife. Even under the Vichy régime, the appeal of the motto had to be quashed with a new tripartite motto: work, family, fatherland became the alternatives to republican thought under occupation. Macron has continued the republican tradition, and has sought to live up to its ideals of liberty, equality and fraternity. Yet one cannot help but notice at the very least a slight rebranding, or, for Macron's critics, a thorough overhaul of those republican ideals. Liberty has made way for a strengthening of the state in its sovereign functions: those of maintaining order and projecting power with a rise in the notion of security. Equality has been defended according to one particular definition, one that promotes merit above all other types of equality. Fraternity has given way to hope, with a vision for a future prosperous France built around the figure of the entrepreneur. It is this particular interpretation of the French Republic's motto, by Macron, his governments and political movement, that is under investigation here. It forms the basis of Macron's ideology, the core values of a new vision for France.

The rise of Emmanuel Macron to power announced a revolution, as his own book/political programme of 2016, titled *Révolution*, attempted to portray. This is an overstatement. Macron's reforms and ideals, taken individually, have roots that make them, at best, incremental changes in focus. Nicolas Sarkozy had already insisted on security as a core value, the French educational system is notoriously highly meritocratic and the pride of politicians on both sides of the political spectrum, and the rise of the entrepreneur as a figure of hope did not wait for the rise of centrism as a political force. Yet there is something distinctly novel in the particular *agencement*, to use the term coined by Deleuze and Guattari (Phillips 2006). It is in the assemblage of these notions – security, merit, hope – that one finds the new political right put in place under Macron's leadership in France.

Against all of the centrist rhetoric out there – and there is plenty – this book argues that it is a new right that is emerging in France, a country where the rise of neoliberalism had been slowed by political values, particularly on the right, anchored in Gaullism and *dirigisme* – a strong control, by the state, of economic and social matters. This new right finds echoes in other political movements throughout the world, but always with a specific French flair. Elements of its security apparatus remind us of some of the age-old conservative arguments about the need to secure private property found in Edmund Burke's thought. Conservatism already demanded security to guarantee private property rights, but it also attempted, unlike Macron's security régime, to safeguard large areas of personal liberty against state interference. Parts of its ideal of meritocracy have already been established in the ideological justification of capitalism and its ethics of responsibility. Max Weber had already shown that a deep theological justification was needed to set up a meritocratic vision of the world, a theological justification that is hidden in plain sight in Macron's defence of French meritocracy. The political theology of hope finds resonance in an economic model that values charity over solidarity. Yet not even the deepest troubles created by previous social unrest in France saw such a systematic repression of the right to demonstrate against the government. No single political movement managed to put these three values together in quite the same manner as Macron has done. This in itself is a fascinating development, a novel political movement that puts together a set of values that resonates with society enough for its leader to be elected and re-elected to the highest office in the land. But this book also argues that this new movement revives and redefines a particular movement of the right: a self-assertive liberalism with neoliberal characteristics.

One common objection to the thesis I put forward here – that Macron is proposing a new right for French politics – is that ideological divides are a thing of the past. Surely, the objection goes, we see the decline of traditional left/right political movements throughout the world, including in France where the two traditional parties on either side of the political spectrum, the *Parti Socialiste* (PS) and *Les Républicains* (LR), have lost large shares of the vote since the 1980s. The picture of a post-ideological world is alluring, particularly in the French context where the French presidential elections of 2017 and 2022 seemed to signal the death knell of old ideologies, as the two finalists came from outside the traditional parties of power. Emmanuel Macron can be portrayed as a pragmatist, concerned with the sound management of the political system, against enemies of the republic, notably Marine Le Pen, the leader of the far-right party *Front National* (FN), rebranded as the *Rassemblement National* (RN) in 2018. While there is a clear decline in the vote for two of the parties of power, it is not clear that this signals the end of the left/right dichotomy, rather than a repositioning of this divide. The vote for the FN and *La France Insoumise* (LFI) in 2017 testifies to this new trend and to the survival of the old dichotomy. At the same time as we think of politics as beyond ideological boundaries, we see the electoral popularity of parties further to the right and further to the left of the traditional parties of power. Muxel (2020, 100–103) shows this difficulty in interpretation well. On the one hand, we have a weakening of people's self-identity as either 'on the right' or 'on the left', and a rise in leftist and right-wing parties. Young voters, in particular, are both apathetic to the political process and choosing more radical choices than the rest of the population. It is better to think of these changes not simply as the vanishing of ideologies, as the withering away of the left/right cleavage, or as the end of history, but rather as the repositioning of political antagonisms, as the redrawing of lines of political demarcation around novel political ideologies. Macron's new right is here not seen as a neutral, pragmatist approach to politics, but rather as a repositioning of the right not simply against the far right (with Marine Le Pen), but also against the left (with Jean-Luc Mélenchon). As we will see in Chapter 1, this shift follows a gradual movement to the right of a wing of the Socialist Party, culminating in François Hollande's presidency of 2012–17. The PS under Hollande had moved so far to the right that it lost most of its political appeal to the left-leaning electorate. Its former members were already split on key issues – the attitude towards the European Union (EU), the role of the state in the national economy, employment and pensions reforms, the use of special powers to push through legislation – with a left/right cleavage inside the party itself. The disaster of the 2017 election, where the party in power came fifth in the first round, with a measly 6 per cent of the vote, was triggered by the *en masse* movement of many of its voters, members and politicians to Macron's new party, *La République En Marche!* (LREM).

Macron's legacy

In Macron's birthplace, the small city of Amiens in northern France, one can admire a spectacle worth the detour on a trip to the country. Every night over the summer, and for a month around Christmas, the medieval cathedral is brought back to its former glory, lit up by a series of projectors enlivening the monument with colours over a 50-minute journey combining the remembrance of the past, when cathedrals were painted with bright colours, with a celebration of the present, with modern techniques to bring us the atmosphere of nostalgia alongside a genuinely novel form of art. The sound-and-light show, which has been running since 1999, is a good analogy of Macron's philosophy of the '*en même temps*' ('at the same time'). At the same time, the spectacle is both historical and looking to the future. At the same time, it both educates and entertains. At the same time, it both reminds one of the religious past and secularizes it. Macron, according to his own narrative, is candidate and then president of the '*en même temps*'. At the same time left and right, at the same time focusing on security and protecting liberty, at the same time defending merit and making us responsible for our own choices, at the same time providing hope and reforming solidarity. A revolutionary who claims France's monarchical past as his heritage, a banker who believes in public service, an outsider to the political system who was a former minister, a converted Catholic who is now an agnostic, Macron is the candidate of contradictions par excellence. Yet behind these apparent incompatibilities, there is a coherent political, social and economic programme for France.

Macron's legacy, at the end of his first term in office, paints a very different story than this philosophy of '*en même temps*'. Already when he was minister of the economy under Hollande, he was responsible for one of the most neoliberal reforms carried out in France in the past three decades. The Macron law, which we will discuss in Chapter 1, foreshadowed what was to come during his presidency – only those who were not paying attention were fooled by his theory of capitalism with a human face. Even before his appointment as minister, when he was a civil servant during Sarkozy's presidency, Macron had tirelessly worked on the Attali Commission report (2008), suggesting widespread neoliberal measures for the ailing French economy. The report, which came out just as the 2008 financial crisis was erupting into full swing, was shelved but still forms the basis for what Macron proposed during his presidency. Two key measures, the suppression of the *Impôt de Solidarité sur la Fortune* (ISF), the Solidarity Tax on Wealth, and the flat tax for revenues of capital, announced the economics of the Macron régime in 2017. Tax breaks for the richest, with a largely regressive taxation system at the very top, was the one-size-fits-all solution to French economic woes. What was portrayed as a technocratic solution to a technical problem was very clearly taking a stance on the right of the political spectrum. These reforms were brought forward at the same time as Macron was revisiting employment law in France, making it easier to dismiss employees without cause and limiting compensations for workers fired unlawfully, once again siding with employers rather than employees. After a proposed new tax on fuel was announced in 2018, which hits the poorest harder than anyone else, the social movement of the *gilets jaunes* fought back against the régime. Just as Macron's rise to power had happened outside of the established political structures of pre-Macron France, the yellow vest movement happened outside of the conventions of social movements and protests. Started on Facebook, without representatives, the structure of the movement was as flexible as that of Macron's LREM. The *gilets jaunes* were, for all intents and purposes, the only political opposition of Macron's first term in office.

They forced his government to back down, cancelling the tax on fuel, and forced it to promise increases to social spending – though the amount of these measures paled in comparison to the previous tax breaks for the rich. The assault on public spending continued relentlessly throughout 2019, and was only halted, or rather put on hold, by the COVID-19 pandemic in 2020. Macron, whose pension reforms are still in the works and were promised to form part of his second mandate during the 2022 campaign, are a fundamental shake-up of workers' benefits in France. Even the response to the pandemic, financed largely through public debt, announces a difficult time ahead for French citizens. Austerity, lower public spending, and higher taxes (though not for those at the very top of the income brackets) are all to come to deal with a public debt that has now reached 115 per cent of GDP. At the same time, Macron has promised massive public investment in innovative sectors, up to €100 billion announced in 2020. Macron also proposed to reform unemployment benefits, making claims more difficult and capping benefits – but his measure was struck down by the *Conseil d'État*, France's highest administrative court. Lower taxes at the top, widespread social protests, minimal improvements for those at the very bottom, cuts and the promise of more cuts to public services and welfare benefits, a growing public debt: this is the economic legacy of Macron after five years in power. It clearly positions him on the right of the political spectrum and dispels the myth of Macron's neutrality and pragmatism.

Macron is also a progressive politician, at least where social reforms do not need much money. The key measure of his social progress agenda has been the opening up of medically assisted reproduction technologies to homosexual couples and single women – though the legislation still excludes transgender persons. Paternity leave has also been doubled under Macron, to 28 days. His social measures are few and far between, further tempered by the law on separatism, which is not progressive by any standards. The law, introduced by Macron and strengthened in the Senate, passed a number of measures clearly targeting Muslims in France, which included the banning of religious symbols on school trips (for accompanying parents), the banning of the hijab in public for minors, measures to ban burkinis from public swimming pools, and the banning of prayers in universities (Public Sénat 2021). The few progressive social measures passed under Macron have their limits. Equally, on the international stage, Macron has straddled the divide between progressive politics and good old-fashioned *raison d'état*. We will return to these in Chapter 2, to show that in Mali and Western Africa, Macron has largely continued a policy of French interventionism. Suffice to say for now that Macron has applied multilateral diplomacy where he could find allies and partners, and unilateral diplomacy where he must.

Liberalism triumphant

In an interview given to the television channel France 2 in November 2016 during the run-up to the 2017 election, Emmanuel Macron made his profession of faith: 'I do not believe in going back to conservatism, nor in a retracted left. I believe in this progress camp. Let's demolish this Berlin Wall, and not move backwards.' Macron, who campaigned on a centrist platform of neither left nor right, had not abandoned ideology altogether but rather had flown his colours high in front a nation in quest of change: his was the camp of victorious liberalism, his was the camp of the future, his was the camp of progress. His unabashed faith in the benefits of liberal ideology resemble those espoused by Francis Fukuyama (1992) in his thesis on the end of history. But Fukuyama's tentative answer to the events of the late 1980s, punctuated by a question mark, has since been replaced by an affirmation, an imperative, punctuated by an exclamation mark. *En Marche!* was the slogan of Emmanuel Macron's ambitions, a personal political movement based on the candidate himself, a political start-up to boost France's entrepreneurial spirit, a self-assuming ideology for the twenty-first century. For Fukuyama, the end of history moment was characterized not so much by the end of ideology or a convergence between capitalism and socialism, but by the unambiguous victory of Western democratic liberalism as the sole remaining ideology. Fukuyama, a Hegelian thinker, was used to thinking in terms of dialectics, the struggle of contradictions to be overcome, leading to a new order. But those who believe that the end of history is the end of ideology are profoundly mistaken (Hochuli et al 2021); in fact the end of history is the victory of a particular type of ideology over and above the conservative/socialist dichotomy. Liberalism plays this role in Fukuyama, and a particular type of liberalism also plays this role for Macron. The fall of France's Berlin Wall, according to this narrative, happened with the election of Emmanuel Macron as the eighth president of the French Fifth Republic on 7 May 2017 and his re-election on 24 April 2022.

The youngest president of the Fifth Republic, elected at the age of 39, promised to usher a new order in French politics. By the time he defeated the extreme-right candidate Marine Le Pen in the second round of the presidential election in 2017, the two main political formations that had ruled France since 1981, the left-wing PS and the right-wing LR, were in complete disarray. After the catastrophic presidency of François Hollande, who did not dare to run for a second term in office, and the Fillon affair that discredited the republicans' candidate to the presidency, the legislative elections that traditionally follow the presidential elections almost completed uprooted the French political class. The National Assembly of June 2017 resembled no other in the history of the Fifth Republic, with three quarters of the representatives having been replaced that year. As many socialists and republicans lost their seats, booted out of their constituencies by the political novices of Macron's rebranded party, LREM, a new order of French politics was indeed organized around the figure of Macron. With over four hundred rookies in the lower chamber of the parliament, the prospect of an effective opposition from with the ruling party became a practical impossibility. With over 53 per cent of the seats going to the new party, and the third biggest party, the *Mouvement Démocrate* (MoDem), a centre-right party in France under François Bayrou entering a coalition with Macron's contingent, the elections of 2017 put the executive and legislative firmly in the hands of the new régime. Only the upper chamber of the legislature, the *Sénat*, remained outside the reach of the political machine behind Macron's leadership – though they used this power sparingly during Macron's first term in office. The Senate, whose elections are divorced from the cycle of presidential elections, remained largely unscathed by the political tsunami of 2017, making them the only effective opposition in the highest organs of state power in Paris. But the French political system has many recourses for the executive to overcome legislative deadlocks. The French Fifth Republic allows a level of control by the president that gives it a particular flair of authority. The most dramatic of the measures allowed under the Constitution, the '49-3' (which refers to Article 49, section 3 of the Constitution), allows the government to impose the adoption of a law, immediately and without a vote. In addition to this iconic measure, rule by ordinances is also possible, effectively making debates in the National Assembly empty talk as the decision ultimately lies out of the hands of elected members of parliament, directly in the hands of the appointed prime minister (PM) who serves at the pleasure of the president. The end of history also signifies the end of politics in the French case, with little or no opposition, and effectively without the ability of politicians to stop individual policies desired by the president – and pushed through by his prime ministers.

Emmanuel Macron, back in 2015 when he was the economy minister, was particularly traumatized by his boss, then PM Manuel Valls, using the 49-3 to push through Macron's economic reforms past a recalcitrant left wing of the Socialist Party in parliament. Faced with political opposition, Macron could not convince members of his own party that his was the best way forward for the country. It was clear to left-leaning socialists that Macron's reforms were too far to the right, and the *frondeurs*, the rebels, made their opposition clear. But the end of history demands the end of politics as we know it, the end of opposition and political disagreement. What better way to bypass the political opposition than to frame reforms and fundamental changes to the rule of law as mere technocratic changes? Macron trained at the elite *École National d'Administration* (ENA), the postgraduate institute created by Charles de Gaulle in 1945 to train elite civil servants, but which also produces many high-ranking managers and executives in the private sector and has given France many presidents, PMs and other politicians. Its notable alumni include Emmanuel Macron, his two PMs Édouard Philippe and Jean Castex, past presidents François Hollande, Jacques Chirac and Valéry Giscard d'Estaing, and nearly a hundred ministers, despite accepting only around eighty students a year after a rigorous and highly selective *concours* – the meritocratic competitive exam which grants entry to France's *grandes écoles*(the equivalents of the Ivy League in the US or the Russell Group in the UK). What graduates of the school know above all else is that there are technical solutions to most social problems we face today. Politics as the art of disagreement or struggle, politics as the defence of ideals and values, is too murky for the administrative science taught at the school. The neutralization of politics comes with an ideal of technocracy, which finds solutions to social ills that are not open to debate and discussion. The imposition of a new tax on fuel and the new speed limit on French roads announced in 2018 which sparked the *gilets jaunes* protests were the key measures of this technocratic rule. These measures, justified as ecologically friendly, cost-efficient and potentially life saving, had not taken into account the impact on those who live in peripheral France, depend on their car for daily activities and employment, and have no access to public transport. The government had to abandon some of the measures, but the technocratic ideal survived the crisis. If politics has left the National Assembly, it has not left the streets and roundabouts of France. The technocratic apolitical stance of elites – which started well before Macron came to power – is facing an increasingly politicized population, albeit not along traditional party lines.

The political start-up *En Marche!* has shattered the existing political parties of France. The old political cleavages, between socialists and republicans, which have largely shaped the structure of the Fifth Republic, and indeed those of previous republics, seem to be a thing of the past. Though Giscard d'Estaing (VGE for short, president for one term in 1974–81) had already ruled from the centre ground, Macron's rise to power has shaped the political landscape in a lasting manner in a way VGE never could. In 2022, the political left is still in shatters, with the PS candidate for the 2022 elections gaining a measly 2 per cent of the vote, despite her party having been in power five years prior to the election. The traditional political right fared little better. With many republicans from LR having switched parties and sided with Macron's new brand of political entrepreneurs, such as the former republican Édouard Philippe who became Macron's first PM, or Jean Castex who became the second PM, the traditional right failed to capture public opinion with the LR candidate to the 2022 presidential elections failing to reach the 5 per cent threshold to get campaign expanses reimbursed. In the European elections of 2019, the largest political barometer after the 2017 changes in the political landscape, Macron's party and its allies came second behind the far-right RN, followed by the greens, and in fourth position

LR, trailed by LFI in fifth and the PS in sixth position. With the traditional parties of power ending up in fourth and sixth position, with barely over 15 per cent of the vote between them, the 2019 elections were a resounding confirmation of the change in the political landscape. Though European elections are notoriously unrepresentative of other elections and one cannot make generalizations based solely on these results, the trend was confirmed in the 2022 presidential elections: LR, traditionally gathering the right-wing vote, have given way to Macron's party, and the PS has lost ground to leftists under Mélenchon's LFI as well as the greens. An analysis of the change in voting behaviour between 2017 and 2019 is revealing of this wider trend. Whereas 39 per cent of Macron's electors self-positioned on the left in 2017, only 19 per cent did so in 2019 (with 2 per cent identifying as 'on the left' and 17 per cent as 'on the centre-left'). While only 26 per cent of his 2017 electors would self-identify as 'on the right', the figure shot up to 51 per cent in 2019 (with only 6–7 per cent refusing to position themselves politically). A small dip in centrist voters, from 28 per cent to 24 per cent, also hints at a repositioning of the electorate (Opinionway 2019). In other words, left and right are not quite categories of the past. It is more accurate to say that left and right have changed party allegiances: that the left has shifted to a more radical party under Mélenchon and to the greens, and the right has shifted from LR to Macron. Practically none of the more left-wing voters backed Macron in 2019, and one in two of those who identify as 'on the centre-left' had left him for greener pastures. Where Macron's electoral positioning in 2017 aimed at the centre, it soon changed to aim clearly at the right – with the centre now a secondary target. Among the new voters of the right that Macron's party captured in 2019, the crucial difference from those who remained loyal to LR was their attitude towards the *gilets jaunes* protests. Eighty-three per cent of the electors who switched from LR to LREM in 2019 'did not support [the movement] at all', compared with 51 per cent sharing a similar opinion who remained loyal to the LR. In other words, the law-and-order approach favoured by Macron in 2018–19, with often violent repression of peaceful protesters, convinced many who had remained on the right in 2017 to come over to Macron's side in 2019. Fears of a soft liberal response to social movements were set aside once it became clear that Macron was willing to do whatever it took to push through his reforms. Macron's security régime convinced many on the right that he was their new candidate, as early as 2019.

The big unknown remains the challenge from movements on the far right of the political spectrum. Macron's discourses point to the end of history having ushered a new era of political contestation: between globalists and nationalists; liberals and protectionists; the party of hope and the party of fear. Elected just after the victory of Donald Trump as President of the United States and the Brexit vote in the United Kingdom,

Macron portrayed himself as the candidate of sensible politics against the extremes. The only political dichotomy that remains, if we are to believe this version of the end of history, is between those who look to the future, accepting globalization, capitalism and social progress, and those who look to the past, clinging on to national sovereignty, public spending and regressive social values. The picture is convenient for electoral reasons, gathering voters from left, right and centre under a common banner against extremism. It was already part of Fukuyama's triumphant liberalism of 1989, and Karl Popper's open society of 1945, to portray the liberal tradition as the last rampart against the extremes of communism and fascism (Popper 1966). Today, it is framed as a choice between Macron and Le Pen, the liberal centrist against the far-right fascist. The only political dichotomy that is left, according to this picture, is clearly a picture of right versus wrong. The winners of globalization are pitched against the losers; those who favour an openness to the world against those longing for a return to the past; those who live in cities against those who merely linger in the periphery. There is little evidence, however, that this dichotomy explains the polarities in place in contemporary politics. To stick to France, a few examples show the difficulties in maintaining this open/closed society conception of politics. During the 2005 debate on the project for a constitution for Europe, which was defeated, the battle lines were not exclusively drawn between those in favour of more openness or less openness, but also on the vision of social policy in a reformed European Union. The Socialist Party was split down the middle over the issue, with Hollande siding with the yes vote, and Laurent Fabius with the noes. Fabius, however, failed to capitalize on the success of his position when the no vote succeeded in the referendum in 2005, and was not invested as the PS candidate in 2007, ousted by Ségolène Royal in the primary. The referendum's outcome was largely ignored and the Treaty of Lisbon, which replaced the 'Constitution', pushed through without a new referendum. The possibility of a new left, centred around a new conception of Europe and a revision of France's international engagements, went from being a concrete potential in 2005, to being a distant dream by 2007. With no concrete opposition from the left, the battle of ideas seemed firmly enshrined on the right of the political spectrum. The Fillon candidacy in 2017 also testified to the complexity of social mores. Close to the Catholic right, François Fillon campaigned on family values and was close to *La Manif pour tous*, the anti-gay-marriage social movement of 2012. Fillon's candidacy, which lost credence because he came to be investigated (and later condemned) for fraud during the campaign, nonetheless showed that social conservatism was not a monopoly of the far right. A considerable proportion of the conservative right abhors the form of social progress promoted by liberalism, without wanting to challenge the values of the republic in the process. Macron's dichotomy of open/closed society also cuts across the traditional parties, both left and right, and cannot just be a dichotomy of the centre against the extremes.

Even the far-right FN, rebranded as the RN after the 2017 election, lacks the courage of this ambition and does not neatly fit into Macron's conception of closed society. During efforts aimed at 'de-demonization' of the party, Marine Le Pen has dropped the political ambitions of a nationalist alternative to the liberal project. If she ever comes to power, there will be no Frexit, no withdrawal from the euro, no Sixth Republic – unlike what her father promised when he was head of the party. For all the talk of national sovereignty, controls on immigration, and national preference, Marine Le Pen's party does not give itself the means to achieve its ambitions. How is one to pursue an independent industrial policy without control of the monetary supply? How is one to pursue controls at borders while staying within a zone of free movement? How is one to reform the country with only mere tweaks of the Constitution? The RN remains a desperately reactionary party, with no programme for how to achieve its supposed goals and ambitions. It offers no opposition to the security régime put in place under Macron, it only differs in its approach to meritocracy by adding the adjective 'national' in front of it, and although its rhetoric is much more anchored in the affect of fear than the affect of hope, we will see that they are two sides of the same coin. One cannot have hope without fear, and the fear of immigration put to the fore by the RN goes hand in hand with a hope for a better future for the French. In short, the ideology of the far right is not the opposite of Macron's ideology, but only a variation on the same themes. Perhaps because of this lack of ambition, the RN faced an even farther-right challenger in the race to the 2022 presidency in the figure of Éric Zemmour. The far-right polemicist, a novice in politics but a well-known figure in the media, ran a campaign that closely resembled that of Macron five years earlier. The insider-outsider political entrepreneur gathering support at a rapid pace threatening to uproot the political establishment is a familiar story after Macron's 2017 campaign. But Zemmour also lacked the courage of his ambitions. His openly Islamophobic rhetoric may have pleased some of his supporters, but his vision for France is equally as uninspiring as that of Le Pen. No Frexit, no withdrawal from the euro, no Sixth Republic either for the farther-right challenger to the far-right. Although he briefly led over Le Pen in some early polls, his novelty quickly faded during the campaign and he finished fourth with 7 per cent of the vote – far behind Le Pen with 23 per cent. With opponents like these, Macron's ideological clash between open society and its enemies fails to resonate with the political reality on the ground.

Those most sympathetic to Macron's brand of centrism will maintain that his liberalism is precisely a centrist position between socialism and conservatism.

This was the strength of Macron's programme in 2017, which could appeal to those on the centre-left and the centre-right. The neoliberal policies of Macron have also been adopted by parties of the centre-left, notably the PS in France, New Labour in the UK, and the Democratic Party in the United States. But it is precisely a move of these parties to the right that has made this particular brand of progressive politics possible. What I call here the new right can appeal to centrists on both sides of the political spectrum. It may have been more appealing for someone who voted for Hollande in 2012 to support Macron in 2022 over a more controversial figure on the left like Mélenchon. With the PS in disarray, Macron still appealed to those on the centre-left who have accepted the inevitability of neoliberalism as a reality of political and economic life in the twenty-first century. Neoliberalism, as we will see in Chapter 1, has indeed been embraced by the left as well as the right. Yet there is little doubt that this constitutes a movement to the right of those traditional left-wing parties. It is the thesis of Bruno Amable and Stefano Palombarini (2021) that the centre-left shifted its electoral base from the working classes to the *bourgeois bloc* – and that this shift dates back to the 1980s. But this shift to appeal to a liberal electorate has also come hand in hand with the abandonment of the working classes by the PS. A similar phenomenon has also happened in the UK and the US, with working-class voters shifting allegiances away from the Labour and Democratic parties. The contention of this book is that this switch to the liberally minded *bourgeois bloc* by left-wing parties has removed them so far from their historical base that it has enabled Macron to create a *bourgeois bloc* party in its own right. Unlike Labour or the Democratic Party, LREM has no remnants of left-leaning politics remaining in it. Whereas in the UK and the US the *bourgeois bloc* remains attached to parties that have at least maintained some progressive economic roots, Macron's divorce from the centre-left has ushered a new era of right-wing politics in France. Macron, though he was briefly a member of the PS, never sided with its left-wing policies. In economic terms, in particular, he was always at the forefront of the neoliberal wing in the party. The social category of the *bourgeois bloc* that joined the PS in the 1980s has now been emancipated from its left-wing shackles and can fully assume its right-leaning political trajectory. In the French case, it can only count on the support of the left because of the peculiarities of the electoral system. Only in a political contest that opposes the liberal right under Macron against the illiberal right under Le Pen could Macron hope for the support of the left. Fortunately for him, this was the political landscape of the 2022 election, and his new right policies were given a second term by the left, which pushed him over the 50 per cent threshold to win the election. This re-election of Macron in 2022 is not a vindication of his centrist politics, but rather the harsh reality of a third presidential election in the past five that has seen voters face a choice between the right and the far right.

Ideology

This book is about the ideas that allowed Macron to rise to power and to rule since 2017 over the fifth-largest economy in the world. Readers who are not interested in the nitty-gritty of academic research methods can skip ahead to the next section, but for those wanting to know more about how I conducted this inquiry, what shaped the research, and how one can do such a history of the present, I discuss here three important concepts that shape the rest of the study: the history of ideas, discourse analysis and ideology.

First and foremost, this book is conceived as a history of the present, the recent past, and its context. Because I am interested in how ideas come about and are shaped by their historical context – both in my work on seventeenth- and eighteenth-century political thought and in my work on contemporary ideas, the methods that shape my work are borrowed from history. Without going into deep debates about the merits of the Cambridge School's contextualist approach, Gadamerian hermeneutics or Foucauldian genealogy, let me just highlight key methods and approaches of the history of ideas that have shaped my current approach. First, the current work is contextualist. By this, I mean that it pays particular attention to the historical, social, political and economic context within which ideas are shaped and emerge. One cannot understand the neoliberalism of Macron without going into the rise of neoliberalism in France since the 1970s, or its influence on important international partners such as the US or the UK. Equally, the profound sociological changes that are happening in France in terms of the centre–periphery dichotomy or the issue of social *déclassement* have an influence on the reshaping of the French polity, and the emergence of the ideals around this reshaping. Perhaps a little more than other intellectual historians, I am also profoundly interested in the economic context shaping the rise in ideas. French industrial policy, fiscal policy, the rise of inequalities and the pace of privatizations in a notoriously centralized country cannot but shape political ideas in France. For these reasons, I have drawn heavily on the work of others to provide a background for these various contexts that shape the rise of new ideas. I have drawn from historians, anthropologists, sociologists, political scientists, international relations scholars and economists, among others. This is the first pillar of my research: a context-heavy approach which helps narrate the changes to ideas happening today.

The present project started after my *gilets jaunes* book in early 2020, and most of the text was written by the end of 2021, with only the Conclusion and minor edits dealing with the events of 2022. Macron's book *Révolution*, published in 2016, formed the early primary text to analyze the ideological context of the President. The book itself, as much a manifesto as anything else, has to be taken in the context of the 2017 election and is not a philosophical text, articulated political theory or series of social interpretations. Responses to it are highly politicized, and its author is not a professional philosopher – although he was Paul Ricœur's assistant for a time and thus has some very formal training in philosophy. But ideology is not merely established in one neat book, written by a politician ahead of an election. I turned to the task of identifying relevant data for this study of ideology beyond Macron's published works, and discourse analysis provided the tools to find this data. Discourse analysis is appropriate here for a number of reasons. First, the study of ideas is a study of discourse, in the sense that discourse is about much more than mere communication of concepts, also covering how these concepts are shaped by their surroundings and shape the environment they evolve in. Second, discourse analysis is used for more recent policy analysis, and offers a practical way to assess how policies and actions by officials are shaped by particular ideas. Third, it was possible to do, at a time of lockdowns and restrictions on travel, as it could all be done via remote access to media, policy documents, cultural representations and marginal discourses. For this particular type of discourse analysis, I relied on the method developed by Lene Hansen in her book *Security as Practice* (2006). The study of the Bosnian War offered by Hansen is shaped by this method she describes so well, defended as a post-structuralist analysis of international relations based on a Foucauldian ontology. Readers who want to know more about this should read part one of her book, which is a textbook of discourse analysis.

Hansen describes three models of intertextual research which she intertwines with each other for her discourse analysis. The first model, which looks at official discourses, has clear objects of study. These are official texts: direct and secondary intertextual links; supportive and critical texts. These were easy to identify for the present study. They comprised Macron's book, his official communications as candidate and then president, as well as communications from ministries, senior political officials in his administration, and responses to critiques by others. The second model, defined as the wider policy debate, includes the political opposition, the media and corporate institutions. The focus here was largely on the media, as the opposition remained weak during Macron's term in office, and the material available from other parties and political opponents was scant, although some of it was included particularly in the Conclusion. Care was taken to access media very widely, from all sides of the political spectrum. I read and analyzed (from left to right): *L'Humanité, Médiapart, Libération, Le Monde, Le Figaro, Les Échos*, and *Valeurs Actuelles*, among others, providing a wide range of analyses from the far left to the far right. Hansen's third model, itself subdivided between cultural representations and marginal political discourses, analyses films, fiction, television, computer games, photography, comics, music, poetry, painting, architecture, travel writings and autobiographies, alongside marginal newspapers, websites, pamphlets and academic analysis. I do not pretend to have analyzed all of these aspects of Macron's ideology. But, certainly, films and works of fictions, architecture and music have shaped some of my understanding of what happened under Macron's rule. The importance of the roundabout as an architectural feature during the *gilets jaunes* movement, the dystopian interpretations of the future of contemporary fiction, the counter-culture music of the *banlieues*, the historical monuments and small villages of France outside of the metropolitan centres all helped shape a vision of the country that transpires in the analysis. With these three models of discourse analysis in mind – official, semi-official, and cultural – the current analysis aims to provide a sense of this rising discourse of the new ideology.

There are two competing approaches to ideology, broadly speaking: the first, taking the definition of Destutt de Tracy as a synonym for a 'science of ideas', and the second being Karl Marx's understanding of ideology as 'false class consciousness' (Kennedy 1979). We can think of ideology as a positive concept or a negative concept along those lines, as representative of how ideas come about or as the expression of political domination. In a typical Hegelian fashion, I will juggle between the two definitions. As Isaiah Berlin (1969) has done for the concept of liberty, I think of ideology as having two sides to it. Ideology as a positive concept is about the science of ideas: the manner in which these ideas come about, are shaped by their context and in turn help to shape this context. But ideology is also about establishing particular modes of rule, often obfuscating the interests of a ruling class behind ideas that may appeal to those outside this class, but ultimately helping cement political and social control over a wider population. The task of this book is to unearth the positive and the negative, to provide an analysis and a critique. Perhaps here my own prejudices, in the Gadamerian sense of the word as modes of understanding we bring to the fore, become more apparent to the reader (Gadamer 2004). I am a French citizen who has lived all of his life outside of France, primarily in Belgium, the US and the UK. Always an outsider-insider (similarly to Macron in politics), I read French books and watch French films, I follow French media and news, but only go to my home country on holiday or to visit family. I have settled in Britain for nearly two decades now, and share many of the concerns raised by Macron about the corporatist and protectionist nature of the French employment sector. I voted for Macron in the second round of the presidential election in 2017 – though not in the first round that year and not at all in 2022. I consider myself on the left of the political spectrum, but despair about the offer from the political left in France. I have seen the ravages of neoliberalism on my own employment sector, higher education, in the UK, as well as benefited from the opportunities it has offered me. I live outside of London, the closest metropolitan centre, in the small city of Canterbury which has given me a particular interest in issues of those who live in the periphery.

I believe, and will defend this belief in the Conclusion, that an alternative ideology to Macron's is possible, although I find it difficult to see a particular assemblage of social, political and economic forces to bring this ideology to the fore, let alone for it to seize power. These prejudices should not hinder but rather shape the analysis that follows as a useful critique, in ways that are also helpful for those who do not share the same prejudices. The reader will, ultimately, be the judge of whether this has succeeded.

Structure

The four chapters that follow, as well as the Conclusion, are structured as follows. Chapter 1 will deal with the notion of the Macron régime, and highlight how it differs from previous régimes of the right. Specifically, it will show that the novelty to Macron's rule is the unashamed and avowed embrace of neoliberalism, defined as the fusing of state power and the creation of markets. Neoliberalism is of course no longer new, but Macron's particular ideology will show that it is a specific type of régime that is being promoted by the French president, where state power is being built alongside a strategy of power that reduces the role of the state. In Chapter 2, we will see how this reassertion of state power is particularly pronounced when it comes to security. A veritable security apparatus, in the sense discussed by Michel Foucault, is at the heart of the Macron régime. While the response to COVID-19 is certainly the best illustration of the security dimension of the French state since 2017, Macron did not wait for the pandemic to build the security muscle during his rule. This chapter will also show that the neutralization of other political actors is an inherent part of Macron's supposed neutrality in politics (as neither left nor right). In Chapter 3, we will see that Macron's ideology is built on the notion of merit. It is in the philosophy of Dworkin that we find the clearest defence of a meritocratic and credentialist philosophy. This meritocratic philosophy, I will argue, is built upon a very specific political theology – around the notions of the calling and grace. This assemblage of merit, ultimately, culminates in the rise of technocracy. In Chapter 4, I discuss the third and final pillar of Macron's ideology – the concept of hope. By discussing the philosophy of Spinoza, we highlight the dangers of hope as a political virtue – as it can easily be disappointed, leading to despair, and thus to fear. In the Conclusion, I analyze the outcome of the 2022 election, and four possible futures for France. In turn, these are: the continuation of the new right, whether under Macron or someone else; a return to the old dichotomy; the rise of far-right populism; and the potential for a new left. These are not predictions, but rather blueprints for how to think about the future: what ideas could be built, and which could be destroyed.

1

A New Régime

Emmanuel Macron's rise to power could never have been just another presidency for France. From the onset, it was clear that Macron's vision for France was revolutionary and drastic, and it promised to shake things up. The contrast with the past five years of the socialist presidency of Hollande could not be starker. After half a decade of *more of the same*, it was time to shake things up and halt the lethargy. The first task of the régime was to institute a new diet for France. Grown too fat, it was time to start thinning the social body and get back in shape for the global economy. This will be the first focus of this chapter on the new régime: to look at the analogy of the diet to understand what Macron's régime is about. The analogy will lead us to strengthen the claim that Macron's revolution was not a centrist revolution, beyond left and right, but rather a continuation of right-wing policies under a new banner. Even though there have been some token left-leaning policies enacted by the régime, I show that it is in fact a new version of the right that has emerged since 2017. Right and left are always relative terms in politics: they referred initially to the position of deputies in the First Republic in France, with the moderate monarchists sitting on the right, and the radical republicans on the left of the nascent assembly. But the right has a long trajectory of catching up with its revolutionary adversary, and the three historical rights in France (the Restauration, July Monarchy, and Bonapartist rights) had revolutionary elements to them as well. Macron's revolution differs from these three, and this will be the second analysis of this chapter. What is the fourth right, promoted by Macron, about? How does it compare with its historical counterparts? We will see that it is a version of neoliberalism that emerges in Macron's ideology that sets it apart. Although neoliberalism is not in itself new in France, having permeated left and right governments of the past four decades, it is a new, self-assertive and radical version of neoliberalism that is proposed by Macron. It aims at the restructuring of the state and differs from classical versions of the liberal project precisely because of this acceptance of state power. This will form the third analysis of this chapter, to identify the nature of the beast: to define the ideology of neoliberalism and its current emanation in French politics. I will conclude by showing that the economic reality of the COVID-19 pandemic made the claims for neoliberalism increasingly unbelievable. Although neoliberalism is not dead – merely wounded by a health crisis it was ill equipped to deal with – it is certainly on the back foot. It makes the task of identifying its ideological basis and structure even more pressing. Two paths for the future lay open: one where the neoliberal project heals its wounds and revives its vision, and one where it is relegated to the annals of history.

The régime as diet

The Macron régime has a two-fold dimension. It is, of course, a type of political agency, an attitude towards the state, and a mode of power. I will come back to what differentiates the Macron régime from previous ones, in what ways there is both continuity and revolution in Macron's embodiment of his rule. But *régime*, in French, is also the word for a diet. Macron's régime is a diet for France, a slimming down of a social and political set of institutions that have, allegedly, grown fat, inactive and indolent. Macron's training régime to remedy the French lack of fitness was clear for anyone to see in 2016, when he first announced his candidacy for the presidency. It was evident in his public actions of the preceding years, as well as his reflections on the state of the nation in his book *Révolution*. It is not through the exercise of power that Macron shifted to the right – the claim here is that the programme, the vision, and ultimately Macron's ideology were inherently aimed at the dismantling of the social state. This is also the analysis of other commentators on Macron's régime, such as Sophie Pedder, who notes that Macron aims at '[t]ransforming one of Europe's heaviest, most bureaucratic states into a nimble, user-friendly public service for the digital era' (Pedder 2018, 195).

Before Macron joined the financial industry with the Rothschild Bank in 2008, he was employed at the Finance Inspectorate following his studies at the prestigious *École National d'Administration* (ENA), France's highest school for civil servants, and a breeding ground for high-level executives of the private sector. Written in the first six months of Sarkozy's presidency and published in January 2008, the Attali Commission report (2008) provides a roadmap for establishing a new economic basis for a lethargic France. Macron, the co-author of the text, speaks fondly of his six months working on it, time during which he worked with the 40 members of the commission, some of whom became his friends or were useful contacts for his career (Macron 2016, 24). It is the earliest public version of Macron's vision – a thorough cleansing of the state of its social dimension and spending was the message of 2008, repeated numerous times since. The reforms suggested by the Attali

Commission report, though not very original, proposed a clear direction: 'the "'en bloc" implementation of a series of neoliberal reforms in practically all domains, especially finance' (Amable and Palombarini 2021, 130). The highly technocratic report's recommendations could not be implemented by Sarkozy, as the financial crisis erupted in full swing with the collapse of the Bear Stearns Bank two months later in March 2008, making broad appeals to the wisdom of the market and its self-regulation politically unpalatable – at least for the next few years. But Macron bided his time, working in the financial sector at the worst time of the crisis, never abandoning the report's spirit and revolutionary direction.

As a civil servant, Macron had to serve the current president. But a period in the private sector gave him the freedom to choose his political engagement and return to political life on his own terms. In 2012, when Macron was at the Rothschild Bank, he negotiated a deal for Nestlé to buy Pfizer's baby-food business for $11.8 billion. Macron had met Nestlé's boss, Peter Brabeck, at the Attali Commission, and pocketed a commission worth over €1 million that year at the bank (Pedder 2018, 40). It was as President Hollande's aide that Macron came back to politics, by his own account, following his desire to prepare the ideas of the economically reformist left and working directly with the newly elected socialist leader (Macron 2016, 26). During this time, he had the ear of the President, often meeting him behind closed doors and having private dinners with him (Plowright 2017, 123). He pushed Macron to increase the competitiveness of French business, no doubt being one voice among many to push for the corporate tax cuts of 2012 (Plowright 2017, 126). The two men were on friendly terms, at least until Macron's grandmother's death in 2013. Macron, who was extremely close to her, felt that Hollande was unpleasant in his words of condolence: 'I'll never forgive him', Macron told Aquilino Morelle after the event (Plowright 2017, 127). When he left the service of the President in 2014, his wish was to teach and *entreprendre*, to create a business, and he toyed with a couple of ideas: an investment consultancy firm called 'Macron Partners' or an e-learning start-up for French speakers (Plowright 2017, 131–2). He flew to California to hold meetings and secure funding, but events brought him back to politics before these talks could come to fruition. A counterfactual future could have seen Macron establish his own business school, lead the online teaching revolution, or put together his own fintech start-up. In a way, his dream came true only two years later, with the establishment of the *En Marche!* political platform, a communication start-up that led him to the Élysée Palace, the home of French presidents. But before this could come about, he was called back to political life, this time appointed as economics minister by Hollande – the equivalent post to the secretary of the treasury, or the chancellor of the Exchequer. It is during this time at Bercy, the Ministry of the Economy, that Macron put together his legal reform for France. Known as the *loi Macron*, Law No 2015–990 for economic growth, a level playing-field, economic opportunity and activity announced the régime to bring France back into shape. Its reforms included abolishing limits on Sunday and night work, making it easier and cheaper for employers to employ workers during the traditional resting hours. It facilitated bus travel, prioritizing the sector over rail travel and thus aiding the private sector against the public provider. It made important changes to a number of regulated professions, such as notaries, driving instructors and ombudsmen (*prud'hommes*). It introduced measures for private pensions that moved them closer to the defined contributions model prevalent in the UK and the US, and privatized some state-owned assets. It finally attempted a first reform of redundancy procedures, tipping the balance in favour of businesses, notably by isolating parent companies from liability for their subsidiaries, and by limiting payouts for redundancies without cause. The diagnosis is clear: workers should work longer hours, including evening and weekends. They cost too much and cannot be easily dismissed. Some professions, those that enjoy special status, should be reformed to be more in line with the market. Public services should be opened to competition, irrespective of the environmental cost. In short, some (workers, regulated professionals, civil servants) are heavy, rigid and flatfooted. Thankfully, employers can provide us with the necessary régime to trim down these excesses and introduce some agility and flexibility if they are just given free rein to discipline those who need it. The reform came at a cost, though: unable to pass it through the National Assembly due to a revolt on the left of the PS led by Benoît Hamon, PM Valls went above Macron's head and used provision 49-3 of the Constitution: effectively allowing the executive to pass a law without parliament's consent. Macron, who had spent hours answering questions about the law in the assembly felt betrayed and humiliated: the law had failed the test of democratic legitimacy, even as it was enacted (Plowright 2017, 150). When launching his own political movement in 2016, he made clear that this type of experience was not to be repeated: *En Marche!* was a vehicle to help Macron achieve his goals and would not tolerate the kind of political backstabbing he had been exposed to in the Socialist Party (Plowright 2017, 195).

It is not any diet that will fix the French high-carbohydrate régime, but a protein-heavy therapy that is needed. Macron's rhetoric could not be clearer. France has had 'years of weakening', it 'lives for the administration rather than the administration living for the country' (Macron 2016, 48), is made up of 'sometimes criminal dreamers', 'puritans', and 'utopians' (Macron 2016, 50), has 'not stopped all of the excesses' (Macron 2016, 56), and has 'let [itself] go [into] inertia' (Macron 2016, 65). A large part of this excessive weight is located in the 'cost of work' (including wages but also social costs), the 'cost of rupture', with ombudsmen singled out as primary culprits for their generous handouts to wrongly dismissed workers (Macron 2016, 123), and 'unemployment insurance' (Macron 2016, 131). The solution is a 'complete slimming down of our system of social protection' (Macron 2016, 133). The French term used here, the *refonte complète*, provides both the rhetoric of slimming (*fondre*) and of revolutionary restructure (*refondre*). The model for the future is that of the entrepreneur, as we will see in greater detail in Chapter 4, exemplified by Macron himself, a self-made-man establishing his own political brand (Llorca 2021). They are those that do, those that act, those with willpower and vision to carry out reforms. They are those who give us hope, in a world where despair is all around. Since they are profit-seekers, they are naturally suited to trim down excess, keep in shape, and build muscle and strength for the French economy to engage in global competition. But the régime analogy also requires another build-up of strength against those that resist the changes.

The French interior ministry, largely responsible for internal security (together with the defence ministry, which has responsibility for the *gendarmerie*), has seen its budget skyrocket under the Macron régime. Every yearly budget under Macron's presidency has seen a rise in spending by the interior ministry, with the 2019 budget showing a 3.4 per cent increase in spending announced even before the *gilets jaunes* protests started (Ministère de l'Intérieur 2018), leading to a total rise of €3.4 billion in the annual budget over the course of Macron's presidency by 2022 (Le Figaro 2021). Compensated by large cuts in the fields of health and renewable energies, Macron's government promised 10,000 new jobs in internal security, along with a rise in the wages of police officers and *gendarmes*. The security forces are not the only muscle grown by the Macron government. Defence and justice spending have also been on the rise, showing an investment in the sovereign state (police, army, courts), while the rest of the state has been stagnant or shrinking. We will come back to the ideological roots of this security shift in Chapter 2, but the trend is clear from the perspective of the changes proposed and enacted. The state, for Macron, needs to shrink, while it simultaneously builds up its capacity to police its own population, dispense justice and project its own power abroad. The core functions of the sovereign state are seen as the necessary muscle to enforce unpopular changes, repress social movements that fight them, and create a favourable climate for investment and business.

If the police, the army and the justice system are the biceps, lats and calf muscles of the state's body, businesses are the core muscles, the ones that give the state its six-pack. Macron has fully subscribed to the theory of trickle-down economics, the notion that entrepreneurs create businesses, which in turn create jobs, leading to a virtuous cycle for the economy. Under such conditions, it is imperative to empower economic actors, to let them have considerable liberty in their actions, so that they can raise the whole social body up with their success. Macron's preferred analogy for the theory is that of the lead climber (*premier de cordée*). The lead climber is the one that clears the path for others, has the vision and experience to lead, and quite literally 'pulls up' those beneath them, while only needing the safety of the rope in the case of a catastrophic fall. Never mind that this has no relation to how climbing actually works – as the lead climber does not 'pull' those roped to them up the mountain, as climbers often take turns to lead allowing the previous lead climber time to rest, and as those climbers sometimes climb together without waiting for the lead climber to have reached the next pitch. What Macron's analogy reveals is a particular understanding of the economic situation of the entrepreneur. Entrepreneurs are conceived as the heroic figures who take risks, reap glory in the case of success, but are simultaneously secured by the rest of society in the case of a fall. It is a particular model of solidarity that we will come back to in Chapter 4. But the lead climber is the figure of the lean body *par excellence*. Their weight is an obstacle to the climb (every extra kilogram has to be carried up the mountain with them), and their often-long stretches in the mountains do wonders to shed the extra weight put on in between ascents. Joe Simpson, made famous for his near-death experience while tackling the unclimbed west face of Siula Grande in Peru in 1985, tells the harrowing tale of what happens when a climb goes awry. Together with Simon Yates, Simpson successfully summited via the new route, but he suffered a catastrophic fall on the descent, breaking his right leg. While roped to Yates, he attempted to reach base camp, only to be lowered over a cliff by his partner who had no visibility. Unable to pull Simpson back up, Yates famously cut the rope, leading to a frenzy of criticism in the mountaineering community. Simpson miraculously survived the fall, making his own way down to base camp. During the ordeal that lasted four days, he shed 40 per cent of his body weight, ending up at 90 pounds (41 kilograms) (Simpson 2004). Macron's dream is not as extreme. But most falls happen on the descent, not the ascent, and his analogy is suspiciously dismissive of what happens when things go badly.

Macron's lead climber analogy puts him in the direct line of succession from a larger movement, which Michael Sandel has called the 'rhetoric of rising'. It is the belief, made clear first during the Reagan and Thatcher administrations, that hard work and playing by the rules pays off, and that those with the talents and dedication necessary will rise to the top (Sandel 2020, 63). We will come back to this when discussing merit in Chapter 3, but for now it is important to put this ideology in its historical context. The Reagan–Thatcher belief in the rhetoric of rising was adopted in a much wider political context. The market reforms of Deng Xiaoping in China, the liberal turn of Mitterrand in France, and the adoption of the belief in rising by Tony Blair's government in the 1990s all cemented the ascent of this ideology, clearly anchoring it beyond the right of the political spectrum. In the United States, the apotheosis of this rhetoric was found in Barack Obama – no one bought in to the rhetoric of rising as much as the two-term progressive President. According to Sandel, 'it was arguably the central theme of his presidency' (Sandel 2020, 67). Macron merely continues this international, cross-party consensus that rising through life is the fruit of hard work and talent, centred mainly around the figure of the entrepreneur. George W. Bush is reputed to have said that the French have no word for entrepreneur. Whether he actually said the phrase, in a comment to Tony Blair, is irrelevant – its central message might as well be that of Macron: that the French do not know how to foster an entrepreneurial culture. The rhetoric of rising has never been popular in France – even Sarkozy's slogan *'travailler plus pour gagner plus'* (work more to earn more) faced ridicule during the 2007 presidential campaign, as it became all-too-apparent that working longer would not see increased remuneration with the suppression of the 35-hour week. Macron's own rising rhetoric is more subtle than that of Sarkozy: he makes no promises to public- or private-sector employees, preferring instead to promote the entrepreneur as the lead climber.

Macron's economic strategy rests on the double tactic of the creation of a favourable climate for start-ups, and a restructuring of the labour market to give more power to businesses. He planned for a revival of French industry through an ecological renewal led by start-ups of *clean-tech* (Macron 2016, 98). 'It is a stake for the planet and for our industrial sovereignty', he warns as presidential candidate in 2016 (Macron 2016, 101). In the face of global challenges such as rising temperatures and economic crises, the actors to save us from our downward spiral are those who innovate, successfully brand themselves as leaders of change, and benefit from public help through fiscal measures and public investment. We will see in more detail what the role of the state is in this neoliberal vision of the economy, because there is a clear role to be played by the public purse, but for now suffice to say that the entire strategy for growth is based on the creation of new businesses that find a niche in state-sponsored areas of priority. It is also the role of the state to educate the public for this new economic reality. It does so through the 'deregulation of the knowledge market' (Macron 2016, 114), the adaptation of French universities to the demands of the labour market, the introduction of 'e-learning' and the creation of 'radically new establishments, schools, colleges, and *lycées*' (Macron 2016, 117). The revolution of the social body will also be a revolution of the mind, which needs the same discipline, flexibility and adaptability as the rest of the country. Sporting competitions are also fought on the level of morale of the competitors, their ability to learn from their mistakes and not to let their opponents play mind games. A strong body needs a disciplined mind to be at the height of its performance.

Let us not push the analogy too far. The Macron régime is obviously not a diet in the strict sense. The social body is not a material, biological and living thing, and the analogy will remain imperfect because of it. But Macron the candidate and Macron the president have both emphasized repeatedly the need for change, the inefficiencies of the French economy and in particular its labour market – too heavy with social protections and giving too much weight to workers' rights. Instead, Macron has proposed to conceive the French recovery in terms of a catching up with global competitors, always conceived in terms of pro-business policies and strategies. Through his lead climber analogy, the leading role of the entrepreneur is firmly established and defended as the cure for all ills. The entrepreneur's needs – a favourable fiscal policy, a flexible labour market, state-sponsored education, research and innovation – are all paramount to this vision of the future. But the régime is not merely a metaphor. There is a novel vision of the right – itself conceived as beyond left and right – that is at stake here. Let us investigate what makes the Macron régime this fourth right of French politics.

The fourth right

The régime painted above is clearly on the right of the political spectrum in economic terms. It proposes a pro-business strategy, a slimming down of the welfare state, and an investment in the sovereign functions of the state to enforce these changes. But this conclusion is at odds with the characterization of Macron's politics and party as neither left nor right, or both left and right, or simply as centrist. The analysis of the threefold ideology proposed by Macron that follows in the next three chapters should convince the reader that we are in fact seeing a new right emerge, and not a centrist political platform (Gamble 1988). But left and right are always relative terms – one is on the right of someone else, never on the right in absolute terms. For this reason, we must turn to the history of the right in France, particularly well illustrated by René Rémond's (1982) seminal work on the topic. Macron himself, in the 2022 presidential campaign, referred to his vision as inheriting two of these rights – the Orléanist and Bonapartist versions, alongside a vision of progressive politics (France Inter 2022).

Rémond identifies three different rights in French history, from the Revolution to the Fifth (and current) Republic. Since we are mainly concerned with ideology here, I will limit my analysis largely to that aspect of Rémond's work – though sociological aspects of his work will also prove enlightening. The three rights are, in Rémond's terms, the *ultra* right, the *Orléanist* right, and the *nationalist* right. They are characterized by the three régimes of the Restauration, the July Monarchy, and the Bonapartist régime of Napoleon III. All three examples are from the nineteenth century, but they illustrate currents of the French right that are still alive today and are not as outdated as one might think.

The *ultra*, or Restauration, right is the first attempt by the political right to establish itself after the Revolution. It is in 1815, at the end of the Napoleonic Wars that this right comes to power and finds its fullest expression. It is ultra in the sense that it is ultra-royalist, defending a notion of social order based on the restauration of the hereditary monarchy, protection for the family against social measures of the Revolution (notably the right to divorce), and support for the Church through state censorship and anti-blasphemy laws – as evidenced by the life and work of its ideologue, Louis de Bonald. The cornerstone of the régime, as Rémond notes, is the notion of *natural order*. The emphasis was placed on the adjective 'natural', as the experiment of the Revolution was portrayed as a brutal cut with the wisdom of the past and the slow and gradual evolution of order under the *ancien régime*, following natural laws. The Revolution is thus perceived as the unnatural, man-made and rapid transformation of social order, destroying the otherwise natural, divine and slow order of the old world. Unlike *ancien régime* thought, though, ultra-right thinking is based on a biological axiom rather than a purely divine world order outside of our understanding. It finds its roots in an *organicism*, a conception of the body politic as a natural body to be preserved from radical treatment (Rémond 1982, 35–6). Although the ultra right's access to power was relatively brief, spanning only the period 1815–30, it profoundly marked the right–left political spectrum in France. The right was no longer merely a reactionary movement against the Revolution (though that aspect, of course, remained), but it established its own clear identity (Rémond 1982, 59).

The *Orléanist* faction that overturned the old régime to establish a newer version of the monarchy which they thought would better fit the situation of nineteenth-century France also based itself on a version of the 'natural order'. But their notion of the natural order was distinct from that of their predecessors. Whereas the ultras believed that 1789 had interrupted the natural course of history, the Orléanists believed that it was the Restauration of 1815 that had interrupted the natural evolution of society. They saw themselves as the heirs to the Revolution (though not all of it), rather than as the heirs of the *ancien régime* (Rémond 1982, 76–7). The monarchy they defended was adapted to the social reality of the nineteenth century. Louis Philippe was not crowned in Rheims – the site of the divine mysteries of the old order – but swore an oath to Parliament and its revised charter. He became the King of the French rather than the King of France, recognizing the role of deputies of the people in sharing his rule. It is a bilateral contract that was established there, between the new King and the representatives of the people. As Rémond notes, 'it is the revolution of the lawyers: a ritual has replaced the other, the juridical formula has replaced the liturgic rite *et antiquum documentum novo cedat ritui* [and the ancient document gives way to the new rite]' (Rémond 1982, 80). It is the bourgeois government *par excellence*. It is a government on the cheap, or in the words of Rémond: 'un gouvernement à bon marché' (Rémond 1982, 84). The French is telling of the market-driven nature of the Orléanist ideology. Government has to be done on the cheap (*à bon marché*), according to the rules of the market (*le marché*). Against the excesses of arbitrary power and government – the memory of the bankruptcy of the old régime is still French in people's minds – public finances are to be run as the bourgeoisie runs its businesses: with prudence and balance. The ultimate virtue of the régime is savings (*épargne*), a sign of this prudential management of the country and the economy, replacing the virtue of *honour* valued in aristocratic societies. The virtue of savings is that of the father of the family, managing France as one manages a household. To cement its power, the Orléanist right relies on two professions in particular: the university professor and the journalist. It is an intellectual liberalism that is born during this period, and one that is hostile to democracy (Rémond 1982, 93).

Bonapartism is more ambiguous than the previous two rights described by Rémond, as it could have been a movement of the left. There was enough in the legacy of Napoleon and his closest advisors to go either way. A popular appeal, a democratic core, the curtailing of the power of the bourgeoisie, the fidelity of the troops, and some anticlerical and republican leanings could have led to a left-bonapartism (Rémond 1982, 107). But the Bonapartism of the mid-1800s was only to keep a few token aspects of this left inclination. It was popular in that it gave the masses some of the things they desired most: a maintaining of what the Revolution had achieved against the nobility; a guarantee of equality against the encroaching power of the dignitaries that had characterized the *Orléanist* period. It is the plebiscite that perhaps best encompasses the difference between the second and the third right. Where the bourgeoisie was sceptical of the people, the Bonapartist right thrives on popular sovereignty as the source of its authority (Rémond 1982, 124). Gaullism is the manifestation of this Bonapartism a century after its first incarnation. It is an ideology of the right that abhors intermediate bodies such as political parties, trades unions and journalists. It seeks direct contact with the people that it aims to know in its 'indifferentiated totality' (Rémond 1982, 284). The people are politically preferred to their representatives, and a form of authority is built on a popular democracy, sceptical of parliamentarianism – features shared with more authoritarian rights. The French Fifth Republic thus takes part in this third, Bonapartist right, and is not in itself the fourth right. Rémond does identify the *nationalist* right as a potential candidate for the fourth right, and in many ways it is. But its unique flirtation with power was under Nazi occupation, making any analysis of its ideology tainted by the war experience. We will come back to this nationalist right in the Conclusion once a clearer picture of the fourth right has been established.

Macron's régime is the apotheosis of the new right. Like other rights of the past, it does not come out of nowhere, and shares features with the three rights described above. Together with the ultra right, it shares a vision of natural order, although its own vision of what it means is rather different, and Macron certainly does not seek to revive the *ancien régime*. Together with Bonapartism, it shares a scepticism for intermediate bodies such as political parties, trades unions and the media. Together with the *Orléanists*, it shares a reliance on the bourgeois class, their economic liberalism, and their business-like attitude to running the country. But Macron's régime also differs in important ways from the three historical rights of France. It does not attempt to restore Church and state, as the ultra right did; it does not rely on the virtue of savings as the *Orléanist* right did; and it lacks the popular support of the Bonapartist right, particularly in its Gaullist incarnation. For all its claims to being neither left nor right (or both left and right, depending on the context), Macron's ideology and use of political power puts him firmly on the right of the political spectrum.

One area that the Macron régime has in common with the three nineteenth-century versions of the right is its fondness for the monarchy. Macron is no king, but he is profoundly attached to the monarchical past of France. Among the heroes of the nation, Macron (2016, 176) sees Clovis, Henri IV and Napoleon – a strange mixture for a self-described republican! Macron (2016, 178) laments the loss of mystery and transcendence in our contemporary condition, the loss of verticality between those who command and those who obey. He is fond of the architecture and furniture of the *ancien régime*, often hosting guests in the *salon doré* at the Élysée Palace, with its ostentatious eighteenth-century golden furniture. *En même temps*, at the same time, Macron has modernized the look of the royal-palace-turned-presidential-palace in the heart of the capital. He opted for a concrete desk designed by Francesco Passanitti for his private workspace, and put up the *Marianne* by American street-artist Shepard Fairey, who also coined Barack Obama's iconic 'Hope' poster (Morosi 2019). For his first address to the newly elected parliamentarians in 2017, Macron did not choose to address them in the National Assembly but brought them out of the capital to Versailles. Both houses of parliament were addressed, in the style of the USA's State of the Union address, within the walls built to cement the absolute monarchy of Louis XIV. The monarchical tone of the presidency was set, and it continued on numerous occasions during Macron's reign. Macron had already hosted Russian President Vladimir Putin at the Versailles Palace just after his election in May 2017, rolling out the red carpet for the first state visit of the former's new administration. In March 2022, in the context of the Russian invasion of Ukraine, Macron once again hosted his fellow EU counterparts at a summit in Versailles, giving his speech in the *Galerie des Batailles*, which commemorates the French monarchy's military victories. Macron's fondness for the symbols and art of the monarchy earned him the nickname of 'the Jupiterian President', after the Roman King of the Gods. The overwhelming use of monarchical imagery and the ostentatious displays of wealth and power exemplify a recourse to supreme authority under the President. They fit with his neoliberal focus on the sovereign functions of the state – the French words *fonctions régaliennes de l'état* replicate the monarchical reference behind the word 'sovereignty' with the regal functions coming from the Latin word for 'king': *Rex*. The popular sovereignty of the Revolution, however imperfect, has largely given way to the royal artistry, symbolism and function of an office that is, notoriously in the case of France, close to that of an elected monarchy, or as Maurice Duverger (1977) argued, a 'republican monarchy'.

From a consequentialist perspective, where we judge the nature of the ideology by its actions, decisions and legislation, Macron is firmly on the right of the political spectrum in economic terms. We will see in the next chapter that these economic reforms have also led to social conflict, particularly when it came to enforcing economic changes through force in the face of widespread opposition. The economic basis of Macron's turn to the right is seen in changes to the iconic ISF – the tax on assets, primarily real estate, but also movable property such as cars, boats, jewels, furniture and some financial assets. First enacted by the socialist President Mitterrand in 1982 after his election, the tax was part of the socialist programme of 1981, before its liberal turn of 1983. It became a cornerstone of solidarity politics, where those who have a large fortune contribute more to the public purse than those without personal wealth. The tax itself has become the battleground between left and right for the past 40 years of French politics, with Chirac abolishing it in 1986, its subsequent reinstatement following the socialist victory of 1988, its weakening under Sarkozy, who raised the minimum value of assets affected by the tax from €800,000 to €1.3 million, before these latest measures were reversed under Hollande. What we see clearly in the battle over this tax (which affects the top 2 per cent of earners), is a useful ethical canary for the left–right divide in France. The left, who introduced the tax, tended to raise it while in power, whereas the right, who abolished it early on, settled for lowering the tax burden on the wealthy in later mandates. Macron's first and most iconic fiscal measure places him on the right, compared with previous governments in France. Macron's abolition of the tax, replaced by the *impôt sur la fortune immobilière* (a property wealth tax), drastically lowered the fiscal revenue from the tax for the French state (from €5 billion from the ISF in 2017 to €1.9 billion from the IFI in 2018) – a measure that earned Macron the title 'president of the rich'. Much less publicized, but arguably even more in line with his position on the right of the economic spectrum, was the introduction of the 30 per cent flat tax on financial income. The measure, highly regressive in favour of the highest earners, is more audacious than measures under other right-wing presidents and PMs. Neither Chirac nor Sarkozy dared to introduce such a fiscal gift to the very rich. In effect, it turns income tax from a progressive line, where the lowest earners pay least and the highest earners pay most, into a bell curve, where those with large portfolios of stocks pay less than middle earners as a proportion of their income. Macron is not only the president of the rich (say, the top 10 per cent of earners), but the president of the ultra-rich: the top 1 per cent whose revenues are mostly financial, with the top 0.1 per cent benefitting even more. These measures favour the financial aristocracy of the Fifth Republic, who live off rents and dividends, at the expense of those without important financial assets – that is the bottom 90 per cent of the population.

These initial fiscal measures for the rich, the ultra-rich, and those beyond were funded by a tax on fuel, which targets the lowest earners more, for whom the price of energy generally is a large portion of their budget. The social movement of the *gilets jaunes* started out as a response to this tax, quickly evolving into a more general protest about the conditions faced by the working classes and lower middle classes in France. This energy policy is further reinforced by Macron's attack on the SNCF, the state-owned national railway company, including plans for its privatization; and by his initial shift away from nuclear energy, which raised energy costs for the consumer in France. Macron here continued the trend of both left- and right-wing governments before him, which favoured the economies of cities (where public transport is widely available, and the price of fuel a less important factor in daily life) over the peripheries and the countryside. It also illustrates a general shift to the right of French politics, where the PS has slowly focused its electoral attention more on the bourgeois bloc than on the working class, more on the cities than the periphery, more on university graduates than those who merely finished high school. We will come back to this rise of the *bourgeois bloc* later in this chapter. The question is whether Macron is more on the right than his predecessors on these economic issues, and the answer is a resounding yes. By taxing the poor and middle earners in order to pay for tax breaks for the rich, Macron has shown that he defends established wealth over work. By reforming pensions, the status of public servants, and unemployment insurance, Macron has also shown that work is not valued as highly as entrepreneurship, ownership of businesses, and accumulated wealth. Economically speaking, Macron has implemented few measures he can claim to be even partially on the left of the political spectrum. Because they are a crucial counterargument to my thesis, they deserve special attention to evaluate their weight in the Macron régime.

A series of measures was introduced in response to the *gilets jaunes* protests that started in late 2018. These are the only left-leaning economic policies of the Macron presidency to date (the response to the coronavirus pandemic will be treated separately). Alongside the cancellation of planned tax increases for retirees and the now politically toxic tax on fuel, Macron's government announced a revaluation of the minimum wage. This reform boosted the French state's contribution to the minimum wage, through the activity bonus it contributes to the lowest-paid workers' wages. From a budget of €5.6 billion in 2018, the state-sponsored bonus shot up to €8.8 billion in 2019. In total, the fiscal cost of all *gilets jaunes* measures has been estimated at €17 billion over the five-year presidency of Macron, although this figure includes cancellation of new taxes as well as new state spending. What is striking here are two aspects of these measures taken together: that they are financed almost entirely by state spending, and thus through an increase in public debt, and their scale compared to the French economy. That these measures involved a rise in state spending may be interpreted as a move towards the left economically, as the left is traditionally more in favour of a tax-and-spend economic attitude. But there was no additional taxing to finance these measures. The €17 billion found as a response to the *gilets jaunes* was entirely financed through public debt and further cuts in social spending by the Macron régime. We will look at three of these measures (labour, unemployment benefits and pensions reforms) in the next section, as they help explain what neoliberalism is. While €17 billion is a non-negligible sum of money, France's GDP is above €2 trillion. Over a five-year term, Macron's increase in social spending has thus been less than 0.17 per cent of GDP per year (once again, excluding the response to the pandemic). Compared with the measures taken by the newly elected Biden administration in the US in 2021, where the spending is counted in tens of percentage points of GDP, it puts the French President's social credentials in perspective. In the US in 2021, a left-leaning economic policy was put in place, with its scale leaving little room for interpretation. In France in 2017–2022, no such programme existed, with only a handful of social measures taken, which were largely compensated by cuts in other social measures. A generous reading of Macron's policies can claim that he has straddled the divide between left and right, precisely because of these measures. But a contextual reading shows that the measures in favour of some solidarity were small in scale, compensated by cuts in other areas of social spending and always taken from the perspective of the employer, with the rise in wages financed by the state.

Macron's social spending was still pro-business in outlook and reactionary in practice, as it was only put forward when Macron was pushed against the wall by the *gilets jaunes*. It came as a response to one of the largest social movements since 1968, and only when it became apparent that the movement would not go away on its own. The small scale of these social measures does not mean that Macron is completely insensitive to the plight of those at the bottom of the economy. Overall, social spending is not against his ideology and conception of the state's role in society. In his book, he is clear that he wants to do more for those who earn the least, and we will come back to the importance of rewarding work when dealing with the issue of merit in Chapter 3. A higher minimum wage financed by the state is an important feature of Macron's ideology: it rewards those perceived to deserve more without penalizing business owners. Without merit, the ideology itself would be hollow and ring false, denying hope for those who buy in to its promises. The measures, however small and forced by the circumstances, still illuminate the nature of Macron's ideology. Where the left introduced a 35-hour week, allowing workers more flexibility, holidays and shorter hours for the same pay, Macron's policies introduced higher pay for a few, rewarding merit rather than improving working conditions. For now, it is important to understand why Macron's neoliberal ideology is precisely based on this increased role of the state in society.

What is neoliberalism?

Let us begin with liberalism as a philosophical and political doctrine. It is notoriously difficult to pinpoint what liberalism is. As a philosophical doctrine, it does not emerge before the nineteenth century, but claims roots in the seventeenth century, particularly in the philosophy of Locke, and sometimes much further back to Ancient Greece. When it emerges as a political movement, in the 1820s in Britain, liberalism is comprised of the philosophical radicals, which include the young John Stuart Mill. As Duncan Bell notes, the term '"Liberal" was increasingly utilized to describe the politico-economic demands of the emergent middle class' (Bell 2014, 693). In France, this movement coincides with the Orléanist monarchy's coming to power in 1830 and the rule of the notaries under the new constitutional monarch as we saw earlier in the chapter. Liberalism, as a political force at least, is thus a revolutionary force, and Macron's book title, *Révolution*, inherits this historical legacy. It is a political force that seeks to limit the extent of the state's interference in everyday life, and in particular with hostility to the economic interests of the working classes. In France, the Orléanist monarchy also extended the sovereign state functions, notably by enlarging the army, committing to furthering the conquest of Algeria, and strengthening the legal order against those who resist against it (monarchists and organized workers, notably). Finally, it cautiously enlarged the scope for political participation, extending the citizen body (to property owners, widening political participation to about 10 per cent of the population), though it is not until much later that liberalism will be associated with democratic thought. According to Bell, it is not until the 1930s that such a combination becomes widespread, and we see defences of liberal democracy as a philosophical and political principle. It is notably in opposition to totalitarian states, both of the fascist and of the communist persuasion, that liberal democracy emerged as a movement. Since totalitarian states claimed democratic legitimacy, liberalism had to fight its adversaries in this context, and put an argument for why its version of democracy was better than those of its opponents. It is through liberty in economic life, as well as the centrality of political rights (over economic rights) that liberalism defined itself in the twentieth century. Against the war economy of fascism, and the planned economy of communism, the laissez-faire economy of liberalism became a cornerstone of the project. Liberalism restricted the involvement of the state to its most limited extent as a reaction to the competing economic models of the 1930s and 1940s.

The limited state of liberalism is not against social justice. We see, in the thoughts of John Rawls (1971) notably, the clear articulation of this liberalism as both a force of economic freedom and a force for social justice. The two primary principles of justice illustrate this well. The first principle, which safeguards, among other things, political rights and private property, is primary. Once we have those rights secured, Rawls argues, we can think about a second principle of justice, characterized by equal opportunities and the 'difference principle', which allows the redistribution of wealth to justify economic equalities. We will come back to this when we discuss merit in Chapter 3, but for now it suffices to characterize liberalism as a political philosophy which aims at safeguarding property rights and political freedom, with as little state interference in the economy as possible. This interference is limited primarily to taxation, to the sovereign functions of the state (army, police, justice) and in Rawls' case, as well as that of many post-war liberals of the second half of the twentieth century, to an ideal of social justice based on a higher contribution by those better off economically.

Neoliberalism evolved from liberalism, and in many ways is merely a continuation of the liberal project. It inherited the desires for a small state (and, as I will show, for social justice) from its predecessor. But neoliberalism is also a term of contention. It has, according to Phelan, been conceptualized as 'a political economy formation, system of governmentality, political ideology, economic ideology, political rationality, discourse, hegemonic project, system of governmentality, fantasy, rhetoric, and affective regime' (Phelan 2014). Though primarily used by the left as a concept of critique, there are also internal critiques of the use of the term as a catch-all phenomenon to describe our contemporary condition. I share this concern about the lack of clarity of the term, yet find it near impossible to discuss the ideological and economic reality of the Macron régime without recourse to the word. Let me be clear about what I mean. Neoliberalism is an ideology and a political movement that has come from liberalism, described as a desire to have a minimal state with some social solidarity, but with one major difference from the old liberal ideology. Neoliberalism has fully embraced the capture of state power and sees markets as social constructs rather than natural mechanisms, to be promoted and expanded with the capture and use of state power. It is, according to Phelan, 'a political-intellectual project for reconstituting the state as a universe of market rationality' (Phelan 2014). The term has also been used increasingly widely, with non-left parties and authors taking up the critique of neoliberalism, especially after the 2008 financial crisis and more recently with the response to the COVID-19 pandemic. I will thus analyze the consequences of this neoliberal ideology beyond the realm of ideas, remembering that even in Plato's Forms (2007), the ideational structures are only useful to understand the world out there.

Neoliberalism is also not exclusively a project of the right. The left, at least in some of its incarnations, has fully embraced this reconstruction of the state and other social institutions alongside market rationality. New Labour in the UK became a force for the promotion of neoliberalism in the 1990s, alongside the Clinton administration's economic policies in the US. Neoliberalism has abandoned the idea of the natural free market in favour of the heavily regulated artificial market. Since the Clinton/Blair era, there has been a proliferation of government and quasi-government bodies intervening in everyday practices in numerous sectors of the economy. Some of them are part of the voluntary sector – we will come to the significance of this in Chapter 4 – while others fall more straightforwardly under government supervision; with a few falling in between (formally independent, but largely dependent on government funding for their operational budget – the notorious *quangos*, quasi-autonomous non-government organizations). The attempt to build a market where there was none before has been a process that has increased the involvement of the state in the mechanisms of organization. Whether directly or indirectly, the neoliberal state builds markets and regulates them heavily, through a web of organizations performing the functions of the state even though they are not formally part of the state structure. Although both in the US and in the UK many of these measures were introduced by parties of the left, they were spearheaded by a 'new' form of the left – the New Democrats and New Labour, and their Third Way politics. A portion of the political left had moved considerably closer to the right in economic terms, embracing the market as a necessary feature of their new politics, and as a way to finance their progressive policies.

In France, also, neoliberalism as described above has been a project of left and right. The shift, between the socialist old guard and the neoliberal socialism of the latest four decades, came in 1983, with Mitterrand's shift to the right. As Amable and Palombarini have noted, it was around the issue of the European Monetary System (EMS) that the break came. Mitterrand faced a choice: either he continued with his monetary expansionist policy and pursued the socialist reforms of his manifesto, or he backed down, introduced austerity, kept the parity of the franc and the mark, and stayed with the EMS. He chose the latter, with the consequence of rising unemployment (Amable and Palombarini 2021, 38). The old alliance with communists was in tatters, and the PS looked elsewhere for political alliances, notably with the *bourgeois bloc* (highly educated professionals with progressive views), to the detriment of its former base: the working classes. This neoliberal socialism is not without its progressive aspect. The introduction of the 35-hour week under the Jospin government seems like an advance in workers' rights. But this measure was itself the reflection of an evolving neoliberal régime. It created flexible contracts for workers, backed up by state funding to cover the gap between the 39-hour week and the new system. It thus introduced labour reforms in favour of employers, backed up by state sponsorship. The presidency of François Hollande was perhaps the culmination of the neoliberal left in France. In his five years in power, he did not manage to pass a single measure to protect workers, their rights or their status. In fact, neoliberal measures continued under his PM, Manuel Valls, and under Macron as economy minister. The only measure Hollande is remembered for is that legalizing same-sex marriage adopted in 2013 (although civil partnerships already existed in France), a measure also adopted by the Conservative government in the UK in 2014. It was the culmination of three decades of alignment between the parliamentary left and the *bourgeois bloc*, with the catastrophic electoral result that followed Hollande's first and only term in office. Polling extremely poorly, Hollande did not even run for a second term, choosing instead to retire from politics, and the PS only gathered 6 per cent of the vote in the 2017 presidential election, coming fifth in the first round of the election, where only the top two candidates move forward to the final face-off.

As Amable and Palombarini themselves note, neoliberalism 'is characterized by its denial of the natural character of the market; indeed, the (neo)liberals instead thought of the market as a social construct' (Amable and Palombarini 2021, 43). In French, the terms 'liberal' and 'neoliberal' (*libéral* and *néolibéral*) are often used interchangeably, as the former retains a much more negative connotation than in English, notably by being seen as an *Anglo-Saxon* (read: British and American) term. The connotations of liberalism as a progressive force for social change are largely absent from French political discourse, although of course they are part of the political practice. The policies of neoliberal governments, left and right, have often been justified along similar progressive lines in France as they have in the UK or the US. The negative connotations of the term *libéral* thus prevented Macron from appropriating it for himself – although surely, as the analysis reveals, it fits the person and his ideology. But it is a form of neoliberalism that Macron defends, as his use of state power to promote his market ideals reveals.

Unlike classical versions of liberalism that seek to limit the state largely to its sovereign functions (law and order; defence; public administration supporting political decision-making), neoliberalism attempts to capture state power and enhance it with a clear goal: to expand market logic, and create markets where they do not arise on their own. Whereas liberalism in the nineteenth century had taken markets for granted, as naturally occurring features of the economic order based on free enterprise and trade, neoliberalism has recognized that markets are created, promoted and justified through state action. One of the promises of the market-centred approach of neoliberalism is that markets create better economic conditions for all, and neoliberals are thus particularly adamant about creating market conditions that promote this image of the economic superiority of free enterprise and free trade. As Chomsky notes, this leads to a dual nature of neoliberal institutions: they are in favour of state investment for actors at the top of the economic scale, and promote austerity for those at the bottom. 'One set of rules for the rich. Opposite set of rules for the poor' (Chomsky 2017).

It is not a lack of commitment to market neoliberalism, but rather the fulfilment of its ideology that pushes neoliberal institutions and ideologues to argue for increased state intervention. Many examples of this trend – to use state power to create better markets – can be seen in the policy advice of the International Monetary Fund (IMF. To take only a recent example, the IMF has asked for a solidarity tax on the wealthy and the winners from the pandemic to help pay for the deficits of Western states during the period (Giles 2021). A temporary tax, the IMF argues, would go a long way to showing that all have contributed to the recovery, and not merely those who were on the front lines of the pandemic or those who lost their livelihoods as a result of lockdowns. The logic behind all neoliberal institutions is that markets are not natural but products of particular policies, and they can be improved to provide the ideal outcome. When markets are clearly distorted by other policies, such as inequalities in international trade or a global pandemic that prevents economic actors from exercising their freedom, then the state's intervention is a necessary mean to restore market rules to the closest they can be to the old liberal ideal.

We can see a number of other areas where neoliberalism has come together with increased state intervention and involvement in economic activity. The response to the 2008 financial crisis was, in many ways, motivated by a similar logic. States intervened massively in their economies, in order to save the artificial markets that had been created but had crashed. As hundreds of billions of dollars were pumped into refinancing the banking industry, public austerity was advocated in parallel. What we see then is not a shying away from the role of the state in the economy, but a very precise role to regulate market conditions so they can deliver on the promises of the ideology. The neoliberal régime is thus based not on a denial of state action, but rather on seeing the state as the enforcer of the fiscal and monetary discipline necessary to bring about market conditions. When Macron decided to spend €17 billion on social measures and abolishing planned taxes, it was in line with the fact that trickle-down economics had failed to deliver higher wages for workers and resulted in a lowering of purchasing power for working households. It is thus not in contradiction with the rest of the measures taken towards the reform of labour laws, unemployment insurance, and pensions taken by Macron in his term in office. The status of civil servants (particularly those working for the railways), the alleged generosity of unemployment benefits, and the various pension régimes in France are all areas that distort the market conceptualized by Macron. They are seen as remnants of corporatist interest – therefore by definition anti-competitive – and contributing nothing to the establishment of a fair market system. These areas need reform precisely to create better markets, just as the measures to raise the minimum wage and minimum pensions are needed to bring about trickle-down benefits for all.

After neoliberalism

The political philosophy of neoliberalism is defunct. Liberalism's basis for functioning, founded on the wisdom of the market, individual liberty, and solidarity for the most vulnerable, has already been replaced with the cooptation of state organs by market-builders, the reversal of individual liberty in the quest for increased (economic) security, and the favouring of strong economic actors over the weak. That is not to say there is no alternative to the neoliberal ideology of Macron and others. Although it permeates many sectors of society, neoliberalism is not without its own contradictions, and a study of its ideological basis will be provided in the rest of the book. Politically, it has yet to be articulated in clear terms, although at the time of writing, there is considerable hope in the Biden administration's reforms of state involvement in economic life. It is too early to say whether this is the end of neoliberalism, and there are good reasons to be sceptical of such discourse. After all, a similar discourse emerged with the responses to the financial crisis of 2008, although they turned out to be hollow hopes. But the ideology of neoliberalism has shown cracks and exposed fault lines. Even Macron had to abandon the language of the lead climber during the coronavirus pandemic. It became clear during the sanitary crisis that followed the spread of the virus that many of the wider claims of Macron's neoliberal project ring hollow at a time of profound changes. The global supply chains that form the ideal of the neoliberal project, where industrial production relies on free and smooth travel between countries on the opposite side of the globe, showed its limits in times of closed borders, national preference for vaccines, and restrictions on the movement of goods.

France, itself a global player in the field of medicine and pharmaceuticals, lagged behind its competitors when it came to developing a vaccine. Two of the French developers of a vaccine against the virus, the Institut Pasteur and Sanofi, could not compete against their international partners in the search for a way out of the pandemic. The Institut Pasteur finally gave up its development of a vaccine, in January 2021, given the availability of other products on the markets, and Sanofi was still working on its vaccine in February 2022, at a time when the French population had largely been vaccinated already. This disappointing French industrial performance during the pandemic highlights a number of issues in French industrial strategy over the past decades that go deeper. Unlike Germany, which maintains a strong industrial sector to this day, and the UK, which has specialized in the financial industry, the French strategy has been much more modest. Despite strengths in numerous sectors (healthcare, automobile, railways, aeronautics, space, electricity, and communication), reports from the French government highlight a lack of public interest and investment in industrial policy (Aussilloux et al 2020). In particular, France has focused on delocalizing production, to reduce costs, rather than building a production capacity at home. France is the ugly little duckling of delocalized work, faring worse than the United Kingdom, often thought to be at a more advanced stage of neoliberal reform. In 2017, 61.6 per cent of France's industrial production was offshored, compared with 51.7 per cent for the UK, and 38.2 per cent for Germany (Aussilloux et al 2020, 5). These figures reveal a veritable crisis of industrial sovereignty in the country. Unable to produce its own vaccine, the French pharmaceutical sector in 2020–21 revealed a larger hole in French industrial policy, one where the state is still involved at a number of levels (as a shareholder; as a regulator), but is either unable to give its industry direction, or is willing to base its decisions on an ideological basis led by a belief in globally competitive production markets – with all the risks for economic and political stability such vulnerable supply chains entail.

Beyond the industrial failure during the COVID-19 pandemic, there was a *de facto* resurgence of the state that Macron's régime had to come to terms with. When lockdowns were announced, in France as in other Western European countries, economic activity stalled and was reduced to a bare minimum. Those who could work from home were urged or forced to do so, while those who could not were put on furlough or continued working as essential workers. The state then stepped in, with 84 per cent of the furloughed worker's salary paid for out of public finances. The massive state involvement in the economy, providing a stopgap between periods of confinement to slow the spread of the disease, seems completely at odds with the neoliberal ideology of Macron. In times of emergency, it is clear that the normal rules of competition and economic practice do not apply. Macron's dream of reducing the state deficit, and redressing public finances on a neoliberal basis, died with the first confinement in March 2020. Many other measures also forced Macron's hand in terms of public policy, such as the direct payment of some businesses' fixed costs, delays to the payment of taxes, or financial mediation with creditors. What the response to the pandemic has highlighted, in France as elsewhere, is that the state can act, successfully, in the economic sphere, with important consequences for its citizens. The retreat of the state is thus shown for what it has always been: an ideological choice. This observation is even more pronounced as it is clear that the state, under neoliberalism, has actually grown. It has just benefitted certain sectors of society (the lead climbers, the entrepreneurs, but also those who have become rentiers) rather than ordinary citizens, or even national industrial production. Neoliberalism is on the back foot, doing battle with a socio-economic model that promotes reindustrialization, shorter supply chains, national preference and full employment economics. Yet it is by no means defeated, with Macron still gathering important support for his policies and actions from an important minority of the French population – the *bourgeois bloc*. They are the ones that will benefit from the rise in the security state, the promotion of merit, and a voluntarist conception of fraternity in the shape of hope.

2

Security

> The challenge now, he [Macron] said, is 'to build a form of neo-progressivism, structured around the ideal of individual progress for all, in a way that combines agility with security... We have to rethink the framework, and undertake an ideological renovation. It will happen. We need to show the way.'
>
> Pedder 2018, 101

The need for security is an essential component of Macron's ideological thought, so much so that it has surpassed the need for freedom that liberalism is renowned for being founded on. Liberalism had been the ideology of *laissez-faire par excellence,* but Macron's neoliberal outlook demands the cultivation of the value of security above and beyond that ultimate freedom to do business. In order to provide security, neoliberalism has fully embraced the power of the state to create markets and economic structures that liberalism once thought to be natural. Nowhere is this shift more evident than in the rise of security as a core value of society. Where liberty was once the cornerstone of liberal ideology, security is the new value promoted by neoliberalism. By analyzing the thought of Michel Foucault, who was writing on security in the late 1970s precisely as the neoliberal state was becoming a reality, we will see that this new value is articulated in the form of new technologies for the management of populations. Describing security as the contemporary deployment of techniques of power, Foucault identifies key features that shed light on the contemporary application of these techniques. Using examples of the architecture of the town, the control of state-sponsored markets, and the management of epidemics – all of which played an essential role during Macron's time in power, Foucault argues that the rise of security is a key aspect of contemporary politics. Although Foucault does not phrase it as such himself, it is the rise of the liberal, and then the neoliberal, state that is at stake in the deployment of these technologies of security. By focusing on the town, economics, and health policy, we see three distinct areas where this state has established itself as the primary provider of techniques to deal with problems of the industrial and post-industrial eras. Instead of a continued focus on security, as articulated under Macron, I show that a focus on safety (*sûreté*) conceptualized as both safety and certainty, is possible and desirable. Lastly, we will see that the focus on security is not just internal to Macron's handing of the crises in France, but also reflects his international strategy and foreign policy – with important consequences internally when it comes to the expansion of military forces.

Foucault's technologies of security

In three consecutive lectures given at the Collège de France in January 1978, Michel Foucault discussed the notion of security as a feature of our modes of governmentality. Foucault had previously studied the juridical-legal mechanisms of the Middle Ages and the disciplinary mechanisms of the early modern period, before turning to our contemporary condition in the form of the apparatuses of security. These three historical stages – the archaic, the modern and the contemporary – are based on a set of techniques of power used by sovereigns and governments to ultimately manage a population living in a specific territory. Let us look at historical examples that fit Foucault's historical classification.

On 2 August 1618, Lucilio Vanini, a Neapolitan doctor recently arrived in France, was arrested in Toulouse. He was accused of atheism, blasphemy, impiety and other crimes, and subjected to the typical treatment for such a dangerous individual: he was imprisoned, tortured and questioned, found guilty of all the crimes he was accused of, and sentenced to burn at the stake. Before he was strangled to death, in Salin Square in 'The Pink City' near the Garonne River, pincers were used to forcibly remove his tongue, which was cut out with a knife. He refused the consolation from the Franciscan friar who accompanied him and died in agony in front of the watching crowd. A small plaque today commemorates Vanini, on the spot where the infamous 'atheist', whose vision of God was too alien to that of the Church, was put to death. According to Foucault's classification, this is an example of the archaic techniques of power used in the *ancien régime*. The execution was public, clearly meant as a spectacle and a display of sovereign power. The message was clear: all those who hold views considered to be detrimental to social order, and to the stability of the monarchy whose foundations rest on the Church, will be made to suffer a similar fate. But it also obscures the fact that these executions were relatively rare, and that such displays of exemplary justice were precisely exceptional, in the sense that most freethinkers and unorthodox thinkers would not face such an unfortunate fate. Techniques of power had to be brutal and exemplary, precisely because the authorities did not have the capacity to catch most offenders.

The systematization of punishment, and the transformation of techniques of power, took place in the Enlightenment and in the nineteenth century. The 'modern system', according to Foucault, is that of disciplinary power. It no longer seeks to make spectacular examples, but rather seeks to discipline the individual into changing their own behaviour. The ultimate model of disciplinary power is Jeremy Bentham's Panopticon, the model for prisons that the British utilitarian tried to sell to Revolutionary France. The principle of the architecture of the Panopticon is simple: all cells face a courtyard, in which a watchtower is built. The prisoners, not knowing whether they are being observed or not, are under the impression that they are constantly watched by the authorities in the prison. The idea is that they will start to modify their behaviour, based on this suspicion of being under constant surveillance. The advent of surveillance technologies, notably closed-circuit television, has rendered Bentham's model operational practically everywhere, from the street corner to the workplace. It has inspired works of dystopian fiction, such as George Orwell's *Nineteen Eighty-Four* (2000), or more recently the television series *Black Mirror*, created by Charlie Brooker (2012), which portrays a range of dystopian futures, not too dissimilar from our present, where technology is used for its disciplinary power with sometimes dramatic consequences. In the episode 'Nosedive' (2016), every social interaction, whether online or offline, is ranked, leading to aggregate scores for individuals which impact the rest of their lives – whether they can board a plane, which wedding they get invited to, their work, and so on. Social media here becomes the disciplinary tool, the ever-watchful eye of one's peers, where individuals create their own self-brands which determine their success in life (Allard-Huver and Escurignan 2018). What was perceived by Foucault as a technique of power, used in totalizing institutions such as the army, prisons, schools, and mental hospitals, has also become part of everyday life in the digital age, with fiction barely stranger than reality.

Whereas 'discipline is exercised on the bodies of individuals, and security is exercised over a whole population' (Foucault 2009, 11), security is thus the inherently political concept in the technologies of power for Foucault, where discipline's exercise on the individual is much more psychological or moral. The management and exercise of power over a population, and in particular over a population's biological needs and particularities, is the focus of the political question asked by Foucault in his 1978 lectures. Foucault expands on this historical development, from the archaic to the disciplinary, by adding a third historical movement he labels as contemporary – that of security. In the three lectures dedicated to this concept, he gives three examples of the notion of security as it developed as a technique of power: the architecture of the town, regulation of the price of grain, and the epidemic of smallpox. Regarding the architecture of the town, Foucault takes Alexandre Le Maître's seventeenth-century sketch, *La Métropolitée*, as the exemplar of the changing needs of architecture in the modern period. In the utopian essay, Le Maître considers the metropole, the capital city, to be at the top of the hierarchy of the social order. With the countryside as the foundation of the state, and the small towns as the common parts, it is in the capital city that the sovereign's power is centralized. For this reason, it must be located at the centre of the territory of the sovereign and maintain an aesthetic and symbolic relationship with the rest of the territory (Foucault 2009, 14–15). Paris, although it is located in the north of the country rather than at its centre, surely fits the bill of this metropolitan area idealized by Le Maître. Even in the seventeenth century, it was five times larger than the next biggest town in the kingdom (Lyons, with 100,000 inhabitants), and today its metropolitan area is still over five times the size of the next biggest metropolitan area (Marseille and Aix-en-Provence, with just under two million inhabitants). Paris is the site of the most prestigious universities, academies and museums, and of the organs of state power, and it is the economic powerhouse of the country. In 2019, before the global pandemic, Paris set a new record for visitor numbers – hosting 38 million tourists. Its central importance as the space within which security is provided was clearly illustrated during the *gilets jaunes* protests, when a group of protesters occupied and looted the Arc de Triomphe – situated in the middle of the most symbolic of France's roundabouts – which was followed by a hardening of security measures against protesters across the country. More than the actual damage to property over that weekend, it was the symbolic nature of the occupation of the central Paris roundabout – the very first roundabout in France – that demanded an increased securitization of the protests.

Foucault's second example of the rise of the security apparatus of the state is economic: the state's increased interest in the management of the price of grain – the staple food for the urban population. Scarcity, Foucault notes, first appears in the urban setting. Although scarcity is also experienced in the countryside in the early modern period, it is much more severely felt in the cities and poses an immediate security threat in the form of popular revolt (Foucault 2009, 30). With the physiocrats, a group of economists that argued that the wealth of nations comes from the cultivation of the land, comes the theory of liberalism *à la française*. Although slightly different in justification than the mercantilist theories of the same era popular on the other side of the English Channel, the effect of the physiocratic influence over French economic policy, particularly in the years 1754–64, was an increased liberalization of market conditions for grain. Based on the belief, found in the work of Abeille, the French economist, that a rise in the price of grain will result in an increase in cultivation, the French government embarked on a series of measures to subsidise exports, allowed for the storing (and thus speculation on the price) of grain, and controlled imports with tariffs. With higher profits to be gained from grain, Abeille argued, a rise in production will occur over time, leading to both increased production and higher prices – a paradox under the old régime. In essence, we see a form of liberal trickle-down economics defended by the physiocrats: if producers are getting richer, they will produce more, leading to overall benefits for the entire population, despite the fact they are now paying higher prices for grain. The security of the state is thus complemented by an increase in freedom of production (Foucault 2009, 41). This seemingly paradoxical conclusion by Foucault, that security depends on freedom, is not quite developed to its full conclusion in his work. Yet his articulation seems valid: the increase in freedom for producers will require a rise in the security apparatus of the state, as we saw in Chapter 1. More freedom for economic actors will demand a rise in the security measures the state has to take to contain and control the population. If higher prices are favoured as a security measure, they will require the securitization of the population, for whom this increase in prices will have important consequences for their standard of living. More freedom, in the economic sense, necessarily means an increase in the need for novel security technologies by the sovereign.

The third example of the rise in security in the modern period, that of the epidemic, is all the more fitting given the global COVID-19 pandemic and the French state's response to it. Let us identify key aspects of Foucault's treatment of epidemics, and the development of technologies of security used in relation to them, from the eighteenth century onwards. As Foucault notes, it is in the treatment of the endemic–epidemic disease of smallpox that one sees the emergence of the new techniques of power. The disease was both endemic, in that a newborn child had a two-in-three chance of catching it, according to Foucault, and epidemic, in that there were periodic outbursts, notably in London, at regular intervals of every five to six years (Foucault 2009, 58). With an overall mortality rate of 12 per cent, it was a particularly lethal disease, although practices of inoculation from the 1720s, and then vaccination from the 1800s onwards, meant that this mortality rate could be drastically reduced and ultimately almost eliminated. This was despite the fact that these practices were not understood by existing medical theory – it was not until Pasteur much later in the nineteenth century that a scientific explanation of their operation was provided. The question for the authorities thus became how to make these practices normalized, both for the population and the medical discipline.

Foucault identifies four different practices of security that emerge around this phenomenon of inoculation and vaccination against smallpox. The first practice is that of observation of those inoculated, with the introduction of the notion of *case*, an individual phenomenon to be integrated into the collective field. Second, the analysis of the data from these individual cases led to a rise in quantitative research, which established the *risk* that inoculation and vaccination had of causing the disease, as well as the risk of getting the disease despite variolization. Third, these risks were broken down in different categories, based on age, condition, place or milieu. It was found that the disease was more dangerous for those under three years old, and for those who lived in towns; and with these observations the notion of *danger* was introduced. Fourth, and last, the sudden worsening, acceleration and increase in the disease was studied, and attempts to neutralize it were introduced. The notion of *crisis* thus emerged from this concern for the rise in cases. These four novel notions, introduced as technologies of security, remain crucial today when it comes to the securitization during the epidemic of COVID-19: the case, the risk, the danger and the crisis are all categories of thought introduced in the eighteenth century that are still part of our notions of health security today. Let us deal with these four categories in turn in the French context.

As reports of the first cases of COVID-19 came in from the city of Wuhan in China at the end of 2019, uncertainty about the disease, its mortality and morbidity rates, and contagion rates were making it difficult for authorities to get a grasp on the phenomenon. It now appears that several cases were already present in France in the autumn of 2019 – although the first reported cases were made on 24 January 2020 (Carrat et al 2021). By February 2020, there were already over a hundred cases identified in France, and by the end of March over three thousand deaths had been recorded in hospitals. On 12 March 2020, Emmanuel Macron announced what was to become the country's first lockdown. The precise measures of the lockdown become clearer a few days later, when Macron announced new restrictions and declared 'We are at war' (Magazine Marianne 2020), referring to the extreme security measures taken in the health crisis. Like in other countries, daily updates of the number of cases were published, together with hospitalization figures, intensive care admissions, and number of deaths. Following Foucault's observations, knowing individual cases, and identifying how they fit within the larger population, was a key aspect of fighting the disease and understanding its particularities.

The second question, again following Foucault, became: What is the danger of catching the disease, and of dying from it? In the early days of the pandemic, estimates varied widely, from 0.1 per cent mortality rate to up to 25 per cent. The judgement of most governments, whether those of China or Western European countries, was that the danger of contagion and death was high, and the mortality rate was far above what was acceptable to the population. To mitigate the danger, the decision to lock down the population, imposing strict limitations on freedom of movement, the ability to work, go to school or generally leave one's home for fear of catching the disease. France under Macron did not differ significantly from its neighbours in most policies against the disease. Where France stood out in this respect was with the widespread use of security forces – the police and *gendarmerie*, notably – to enforce these security measures. Every trip outside one's home required a separate form, the *attestation de déplacement dérogatoire*, giving the form holder a series of options to justify their journey. Among the accepted justifications were: work that could not be done remotely, shopping for basic necessities, journeys for health reasons or to attend to vulnerable family members, or for physical activity. The fine for failure to produce the form on demand by a security officer was €135, and up to 100,000 security officers were mobilized to enforce the measure (Cossardeaux 2020). In October 2020, during the second lockdown, the form was extended, giving up to nine valid reasons to leave one's home, and asking for the date and time of departure, with time and distance limitations on allowed trips, notably for physical exercise. Numerous complaints were raised with the IGPN (the police disciplinary body), alleging excessive use of force by security officers enforcing the lockdown, including for assault, use of pepper spray on the face, strangling, and use of taser guns during this period. Human rights organizations condemned discriminatory and abusive use of force in the implementation of lockdown measures, and widespread illegal conduct, including racial and homophobic abuse by security forces deployed with impunity (Syndicat des Avocats de France 2020). The case of Michel Zecler, a video producer returning home in the seventeenth *arrondissement* of Paris, illustrates the use of heavy-handed security measures during the lockdowns. In a video captured by his security camera, we see the Black man enter his home before being violently assaulted by police officers without warning. Three men are seen attacking Zecler as soon as he enters the front door. They attempt to forcibly remove the man from his home, which doubled as his music studio, before closing the door behind them, punching, kicking and using their batons on the man, while racially abusing him. The police officers claim that the man attempted to grab their gun and hit them, although the video shows no signs of violent struggle from Zecler. Music artists who were recording at the house intervened after hearing the man call for help, and the police left the premises. The officers then called for reinforcements, attempted to force their way back into the house by breaking the door, and used a teargas grenade that they threw into the house. Scared for his life, Zecler surrendered, before being beaten up by police officers in the street, a scene which can be observed on a video captured by neighbours. He then spent 48 hours in a cell awaiting his fate. Saved by his own use of disciplinary power – a video camera which recorded the entrance to the music studio – Zecler was the direct recipient of security power dispatched to fight COVID-19. Following the events, the three police officers were suspended once video evidence of their interpellation inside the house contradicted their version of events (Ricotta 2020). This highly publicized example simply illustrates the cost of the security measures meant to contain the risk of the disease. The administrative forms, and the enforcement of confinement rules by security forces, imply the threat of the use of force, with the dramatic consequences seen here when cases go wrong. In his debut album in 1975, the French musician Renaud denounced the use of police violence during a demonstration near the metro station Charonne against the war in Algeria in 1962 where eight people died and hundreds were wounded. The state-organized massacre came in the context of a failed *coup d'état* in 1961, pressures from extreme-right groups in the security forces, and a militant Communist Party at home (Ollion 2007). France was at war, and if Macron is to be believed, it has now been at war against COVID-19 since 2020 – and at war in Ukraine since 2022. These wars create permanent enemies, at home and abroad – communists in 1962, *gilets jaunes* in 2018, pedestrians during lockdowns in 2020.

Identifying the risk from early cases was a notoriously difficult exercise. In Foucault's analysis, the risk is more linked to the practice of inoculation or vaccination, as the risk to those vaccinated must be weighed against the danger of the disease. We have already noted in Chapter 1 that the French industrial complex came up short when it came to providing a vaccine. Whereas China, Russia, the UK, the US, the Netherlands and Germany all played a prominent role in developing and manufacturing their vaccines, the otherwise notoriously state-of-the-art French pharmaceutical industry had to abandon or delay two separate projects for vaccines. In a globalized economy, this type of dependence on foreign technology and manufacturing was considered normal, but in the context of border closures during the pandemic it raised important security fears in France. While French manufacturers were able to produce vaccines under licence, the question of who would be able to receive the vaccines first was an important question for the French authorities. Macron's response, unsurprisingly, was to reach European-level agreements on securing supply. Macron did not delegate full authority to the European Commission or the European Medicines Agency, however, and soon claimed the title of chief epidemiologist in France. Where Macron argued that listening to experts was essential in the early days of the crisis in March 2020, he later made it clear that he was reading scientific journals himself, and sometimes overruling the advice of his chief scientists. As early as May 2020, Macron reopened schools against advice from his scientific advisers, who were arguing for a delay until September (Lemarié 2021). In January 2021, when the scientific council was advising a new lockdown in some regions, the executive opted to take a different position: a curfew from 6 pm which relied on the use of security forces for its enforcement (Vilars 2021). Hundreds of thousands of police checks took place and tens of thousands of fines of €135 each were issued, some of them issued to motorists who missed the deadline because they were stuck in traffic caused by police controls (Comte 2021). It is, of course, ultimately a political decision that Macron and his government had to make about the precise measures to mitigate the risk of new infections. As elected officials it was their responsibility to make the decision, and it was within their power to overrule Macron's scientific council. What is striking here is not that Macron went against the advice of his scientific advisers, but rather that he justified these derogations from the rule of experts by claiming to be more of an expert himself. We will come back to the notion of technocracy in Chapter 3, but here it suffices to note that when it came to risk, Macron become the self-appointed expert, taking decisions not in terms of political choices – in terms of balancing civil liberties against medical decisions, for example – or for economic reasons – the importance of keeping the economy afloat versus containing the spread of the disease – but rather as a better epidemiologist than his team of scientists.

It is through the notion of crisis (one is tempted to say, of permanent crisis), that the presidency of Macron is best analyzed. This notion is barely touched on by Foucault, but is picked up at length by Giorgio Agamben's (2005) analysis of the state of exception. Agamben provides us with a genealogy of this legal/extra-legal framework, which he sees as both internal and external to the law. Already existing in Ancient Rome and throughout the Middle Ages, it is in the French Revolution that, according to Agamben, the modern notion of the state of exception/state of war is born (Humphrys 2006). With a decree of the national constituent assembly in 1789, the state of peace is distinguished from the state of war by the transfer of political power to a military commander. The 1958 French Constitution, establishing a state of siege, replicates this provision. Macron inherited a state of emergency from his predecessor when he took the office of President in 2017, and this had been in place since 2015 following terror attacks in the capital that killed 130 people. Macron had been critical of this state of emergency in his campaign, and ended it two years after it was enacted by his predecessor. But rather than ending the emergency, the law which replaced the state of emergency enshrined many of its measures into normal state powers. Needless to say, this internalizing of the state of exception into law led to significant restrictions on civil liberties and a considerable strengthening of arbitrary power exercised by state officials. Powers transferred to local prefects included the right to establish security zones, restricting access to these areas; to ban someone from entering their *département*; to close down public spaces, including concert halls; to forbid gatherings considered to create disorder; to enforce the wearing of electronic bracelets by individuals under surveillance; and to allow searches at a suspect's home without a judge's consent. These measures were widely used from 2017 onwards, not only to combat terrorism, but also in the repression of the *gilets jaunes* movement and in containing environmental protests. An unending crisis, using techniques of power that make the state of exception permanent, became the *leitmotif* of Macron's security strategy – even before the COVID-19 pandemic made this a reality in other countries. This state of exception was further extended during the pandemic, re-baptized as the sanitary state of exception (*état d'urgence sanitaire*) in 2020. Even if Agamben had slightly overplayed his hand when he argued that the state of exception was a permanent feature of life since the Second World War, one can argue that it has become less exceptional since the rise of neoliberalism, and in France's case, at least, has increased in intensity as neoliberalism has strengthened.

Neutralization

The Macron régime showed a particularly heavy-handed approach to security through the use of heavy fines, police crackdowns, and at times the outright use of excessive force, as well as a particular technocratic approach to the handling of the pandemic. To understand how the use of these technologies of security fit into the specific ideology of the régime the notion of neutralization needs to be introduced, because it illustrates how one of Macron's central values as a presidential candidate, his neutrality on the political spectrum, presupposed this security shift. It is ironic that precisely the notion of neutrality, used to understand Macron's rule as non-ideological, can be used in the opposite manner. In his book on the Macron brand, Raphaël Llorca argues that the communication of the candidate Macron was based on pushing forward this notion of neutrality to escape traditional party allegiances and ideology. The very notion of the political brand, according to Llorca (2021, 22), was the system of political representation most adequate for bypassing the left–right political cleavage. The brand, for Llorca (2021, 14), is a semiotic system, a series of signs meant to produce meaning. As opposed to marketing, which aims to promote products, to position them in a market and to compete with other products, the brand aims to communicate beliefs, symbolic meaning, and the imaginary. When looking at Macron's political brand, although Llorca never says so himself, one is looking at the exterior signs of ideology. What the brand aims to reflect is precisely the system of values and the vision for the future of the brand itself. Whether it is Apple or Macron, what is being sold is not merely a product, but an entire vision for the world, a system of ideas and beliefs which regulates our understanding of reality – an ideology. According to Llorca (2021, 23), there are three levels to Macron's branding: an axiological level, reflecting its fundamental values and vision of the world; a narrative level, comprised of storytelling, a grammar and particular figures; and an aesthetic level that includes its logo, visual identity, scenography and symbolic uses, discourse and rhetoric.

The axiological level of the Macron brand is exemplified by its value of neutrality. Using the philosophy of Roland Barthes, Llorca (2021, 26–27) argues that 'the Neutral [*le Neutre*]' is at the centre of Macron's axiological positioning. Neither left nor right, neither proposing continuity nor discontinuity, neither revolution nor conservation, neither ancient nor modern, Macron situates himself in this 'Neutral' that seeks to avoid and suspend conflict. The Neutral, in Barthes' thought, is not a quest for synthesis, however. One might imagine that this refusal of traditional categories of politics could lead to a desire to get past them, to incorporate their most essential features and to recombine them into something new. This was, after all, the strategy of other leaders who were at the forefront of the neoliberal turn in the 1990s, such as Tony Blair and Bill Clinton. Both proposed a Third Way that was meant to get past the limitations of left and right, by turning them into something new. But instead of this dialectic, Macron's ideology follows Barthes, where the Neutral is a form of juggling of two contradictions without resolution, without the destruction/overcoming aspect to enable a more dialectic approach. Harnessing support from all sides of the political spectrum, without any promise of overcoming their divisions, the neutral stance of Macron as a candidate was to propose a vision, a tale, a will, rather a political programme (Macron 2016). For the brand itself, this neutral stance built a certain myth of France, based on its 'monarchical unconscious' (Llorca 2021, 34) that we already discussed in Chapter 1, a vision of power exercised vertically, fascinated by figures such as Napoleon and de Gaulle. The figure of the entrepreneur, which we will come back to in Chapter 4, and of the political *start-up* also acquired fundamental importance in this neutral stance. The entrepreneur is a figure of neutrality: they need to be both a utopian and a pragmatist, to convince with words and numbers, to *pitch* their ideas to investors and to pursue their ideals (Llorca 2021, 37). The entrepreneur is a creator and problem-solver – almost a guru, at the head of a sect. Macron himself commented on this just after this election: 'After, I almost became a sect ... and in the end we did it!' (Llorca 2021, 41). In its discourse, the Macron brand was also seeking this neutrality: Macron used intransitive verbs, as well as transitive verbs in an intransitive manner. For example, his uses of the verbs '*faire*' (to do) and '*transformer*' (to transform) were often used without an object. What is to be done? What is to be transformed? The content, in a way, is irrelevant to the figure of the Neutral that Macron wanted to convey. The important thing was to do and to transform, not what is to be done or to be transformed. Even Macron's movement's logo was designed with this neutrality in mind. No rose as with the socialists, no 'blue, white and red' as with the Republicans, no flame as in the Front National – merely a scribbled 'En Marche!', in Macron's handwriting, establishing a movement sharing his initials. Even the choice of colour for official communications – blue – is taken by Llorca (2021, 64) to be the neutral colour *par excellence,* a calming, pacifying colour that secures and assembles. The neutrality of the candidate was established along the three main axes of the brand: its axiological level as neither left nor right, its narrative level through its specific intransitive language, and its aesthetic level with its logo.

Once elected, the neutral stance of the candidate could not survive political action. A shift occurred, for Llorca, from the neutral to neutralization. The neutral gives way to neutralizing violence, the enforcement of the doing and transforming promised by the candidate. What Llorca does not see, however, is that this logic of neutralization was always already part of the candidate's thought. Those who resist change, those who stand to lose from reforms, were always in need of neutralizing for the candidate's vision to take effect. *Pace* Llorca, the neutral thus comes as a form of obfuscation rather than as a genuine desire to bypass conflict. Conflict was always built into the enforcement of the ideology of action and change. Llorca identifies a triple neutralization: political, governmental and mediatic. Political neutralization came as a result of the landslide victory by the new party LREM, at the legislative elections just after the presidential election in 2017. The old political establishment was effectively wiped out at the level of the National Assembly. The neutral was established as the only alternative to combat the far right – the only party of 'Good' to overcome the 'Evil' of Marine Le Pen's followers. There is no alternative under the neutralizing Macron régime as it rises to power in 2017. Macron or fascism – that is the choice as portrayed during the campaign leading up to the presidential election in 2017, and again in 2022. With politically inexperienced members of civil society being given ministerial posts in 2017, and their actions limited only by presidential decree, it was a straightforward neutralization of ministerial power – coupled with a weak National Assembly – that led to a weakening of the means to oppose the executive. Macron also introduced a spoils system *à la française*, importing this practice from the US where top posts in the administration and civil service are subject to appointment and change by elected officials – or in this case, by the President (Berdah 2020). Unlike in the United States, where many appointments are subject to control by the Senate, there was no such separation of powers introduced in France, with privileges resting firmly in presidential hands. It is the office of the prefect that has been most affected by this change in the nomination of civil servants – for they are the representatives of the state at the local level, and notably for security purposes. Prefects coordinate the police and *gendarmerie* forces, and their appointment by Macron is meant to reinforce his security strategy, with loyalists appointed to key posts. Having transferred some of the powers of the state of exception to the office of the prefect, Macron ensured the security apparatus was firmly within his control. The appointment of Didier Lallement as prefect of Paris in 2019, at the height of the *gilets jaunes* protests, reflected this security shift enforced by a neutralizing of the civil service's neutrality. Lallement replaced Michel Delpuech, who had been openly critical of cronyism at the level of the executive following the Benalla affair, where the President's bodyguard was observed hitting protesters at a May Day demonstration – despite not being employed by the police (Jacob 2018). Finally, neutralization occurred at the mediatic level, where restrictions to journalists' access to the executive were imposed, in order to better control the message of the régime – notably by employing the agency Bestimage to control the executive's brand (Llorca 2021, 76).

It is ultimately in the Macron brand's handling of COVID-19 that the final phase of neutralization is visible, for Llorca (2021, 116). The rhetoric of war, using the terms 'we are at war', 'front', 'first line' and 'mobilization', became part of the communicative strategy of the executive. It is this framing of the pandemic as a war that follows the neutralizing discourse. If we think in terms of bellicose metaphors, we think of general mobilization and the withering away of political activity. Whoever says war says national union, the closing of ranks, and the silencing of opposition voices. Whoever says war says exceptional measures, legislation by decree, state of emergency, massive restrictions to civil liberties, and a rise of the bureaucracy to enforce the measures (Llorca 2021, 119). The movement from the Neutral to the neutralized state, after five years of the Macron régime, is well under way. We have seen that Macron did not wait for the COVID-19 pandemic to initialize this neutralization – his rhetoric from the campaign already pointed to a battle between open society and its enemies – LREM or the FN. In the campaign for the 2022 elections, such rhetoric was again mobilized against Marine Le Pen and Éric Zemmour, as the overwhelming majority of polls suggested a new face-off between a far-right candidate and Macron in the second round of the election. When placing the debate over the topic of security, when shifting the rhetoric towards the neutralization of enemies, it is unsurprising that the debate becomes one between the right and the far right. The far right, after all, has been focusing on these themes for decades. Jean-Marie Le Pen, Marine's father, had run his political campaign for regional elections in 1992 on the slogan 'Security ... first among liberties' (*La sécurité ... Première des libertés*). In a competition over security, Macron is always playing catch-up with those on his right flank.

Sûreté as safety and certainty

For Foucault, the technologies of security as they emerge in the eighteenth century are an answer to the problem of the town: the architecture of public spaces, the management of food supplies, and the control of epidemics are all urban problems to be dealt with using these new techniques of management. Before that time, say in the Renaissance thought of Machiavelli (2003), the question is not one of security, but rather of *sûreté*. *Sûreté*, translated as safety – but left in the original French, in brackets, in translations of Foucault's work – has a complex meaning. In addition to its meaning as safety, it also means certainty – to be sure of the outcome of one's actions. For the purpose of this chapter, I will used *sûreté* to mean both safety and certainty, both the quest for a safe environment and the attempt to secure levels of certainty appropriate to the level of analysis. Machiavelli's problem, according to Foucault, is precisely framed in terms of *sûreté* in that it is the question of acquiring and maintaining the state that is at stake in the Florentine's thought. How can one be reasonably sure, reasonably certain, that one's actions will lead to the consolidation of power? These questions form an important part of the interrogation in *The Prince*. The move towards security as the management of a population is alien to the sixteenth century, but *sûreté*, as the quest for certainty and safety is central to the task of governing.

To reach into the potential of *sûreté* versus security, one has to look beyond Foucault, for whom *sûreté* is merely an early modern or pre-modern *Weltanschauung*. It is in the thought of Paul-Henri Thiry, Baron d'Holbach, that one finds a clear articulation of the notion of *sûreté* in a modern context – as a critique of security understood as the primary task of the sovereign. In the thought of the eighteenth-century materialist, *sûreté* is framed as the counterpoint to property – it is the certainty to be able to enjoy the fruits of one's labours (Holbach 1999, 252). In the *ancien régime*, the arbitrariness of property relations was an endemic feature of political power, with property always subject to the will of the sovereign – through forced taxation, for example. For Holbach, who had inherited his title of baron from his uncle – himself ennobled in his lifetime after gaining considerable fortune – the question of *sûreté* is less one of defending the established *noblesse* than a demand for economic equality. If *sûreté* is enjoyed by all at the same level, as Holbach argues, it demands that people are able to acquire a certain degree of certainty about their economic future. Holbach's answer, characteristic of his bourgeois outlook, was thus to enlarge the body of citizens – meaning property owners – who would then be able to use their land to produce their own goods, and acquire relative certainty when it came to their future economic well-being. Economic independence, in other words, was Holbach's answer to the question of *sûreté*. Safety and certainty in economic life are as important today as they were in the eighteenth century, although the context has changed dramatically. The agrarian ideal of Holbach may no longer be viable in a post-industrial economy, but the principles remain important to many in their everyday life. The ability to be productive, to have relative certainty against the accidents of life, to not depend on the arbitrary will of others for one's economic well-being, are all principles which show the importance of *sûreté* in the contemporary context.

Macron's security turn completely eclipsed this need for safety and certainty in the first three years of his presidency. A straightforward defence of property rights – particularly for the 1 per cent of top earners – was promoted over and above the needs of the bottom 99 per cent. Macron himself has phrased his preference for an individualized conception of security over and above the provision of welfare in an interview with Sophie Pedder (2018, 194). '"The term *Etat-providence* [welfare state] has a maternal connotation, one of hyper-protection, one that disempowers, that I'm not found of," Macron told me [Pedder] in July 2017. "I would rather talk of a state that offers security, that makes things possible, that gives autonomy. That's what I want to do."' Security rather than safety, autonomy rather than certainty, became the ideological roots of the régime. Historically, the concept of *sûreté* has been a powerful driver towards social solidarity, and not only on the left of the political spectrum. Before the French Revolution, in a largely rural society, solidarity was provided by the extended family and the Church. The French Revolution, which shook the institutions of the Church and the family, and the Industrial Revolution, which continued this dismantling of social structures of solidarity throughout the nineteenth century, further eroded solidarity as a political principle. It was not until the 1930s in France that the rise of the welfare state appeared to replace these structures of solidarity, providing a sense of safety and redistribution fit for the new social and economic realities. What may come as a surprise today is that these changes were not brought about by the political left, which was still divided between revolutionaries, who had no interest in making capitalism more palatable to the masses, and reformists, who sought slow and incremental changes. In France, it was right-wing governments that introduced social security – following the trend set by Germany, where Bismarck had already instituted social welfare reforms in the 1880s, and Britain, where Liberals were prominent in the development of the welfare state in the 1910s. When the left-wing Front Populaire arrived in power in 1936, health, maternity, disability, death and old-age insurance had already been introduced, and the socialists and communists who took part in the coalition governments of the post-war period merely expanded those in 1945–46. In France, it was under the right, once again, that the welfare state grew in the 1960s and 1970s. When Mitterrand came to power in 1981, he tried to expand social welfare quite dramatically, raising many entitlements by 25 per cent and some by 50 per cent, but the reforms were short-lived, with hyperinflation and economic stagnation forcing the government to change tack (Ambler 1991). Since 1983, the welfare state has largely been in retreat, and although some portions of it still enjoy healthy public support, increased concern over the costs of pensions and family allowances, in particular, divides the French public (La Sécurité Sociale 2021).

The attack on the French welfare state has been more or less sustained since the 1980s, under both right- and left-leaning governments. Macron's focus on security, particularly through the sovereign functions of the state, continued this trend. Safety as certainty only came back with Macron in response to the COVID-19 pandemic. With widespread furloughing of workers to limit the spread of the disease, it was the state that stepped in to provide secure wages for those who lost their ability to work. It showed cracks in the system of security, highlighted previously, that had been favoured by Macron since his election to power in 2017. It soon became apparent that the state could step in not only to maintain market relations, but also to favour economic certainty for the whole population. Although these measures were largely financed through public borrowing – raising further questions about the long-term economic inequalities this will create – they nevertheless showed the importance of *sûreté* in public policy. Macron, *malgré lui* (in spite of himself), reintroduced a dose of *sûreté* in his public policies. This showed that the state can do more: that it can provide for safety and certainty in the field of economic life, and is not merely a facilitator of market relations. The question of who is to pay for the exceptional economic measures, however, remains open for debate. As economist Thomas Piketty has argued, these levels of public debt – estimated at 125 per cent of GDP in France at the end of 2021 (Le Monde 2021) – are still within acceptable limits in the historical context. Much higher levels of public debt have been dealt with in the past – up to 200 per cent of GDP in Britain at the end of the Napoleonic Wars and 250 per cent after World War II – with numerous policy instruments available to governments to reduce it, including debt restructure, inflation and exceptional taxation of wealth (Piketty 2013). Even the IMF (otherwise not known for its left-leaning policies), as we have already seen, has suggested that taxing the winners of the COVID-19 economy would go a long way to demonstrate solidarity in the response to the economic crisis that will follow the lockdowns. It need not be left to future generations to deal with the economic consequences of COVID-19 policies through debt repayments, as alternatives exist today to mitigate the worst of these effects. Macron's focus, thus far, has been to secure international support for his deficit-financed policies, by getting European partners – in particular, Germany – to support a flexibility in European rules about state borrowing. The political bargaining about who is to pay for the recovery is yet to be done, with few indications that the burden of the debt will be shared equally or through a progressive taxation system. The ultimate test of the Macron régime will be, beyond 2022, who is to pay for the COVID-19 debt. Based on the value of security promoted by Macron since 2016, one expects a strict defence of private property rights (of debt owners and the economic winners of the pandemic) over the safety and certainty of the rest of the population. Piketty's policy instruments to deal with public debt would weaken the security of property owners, and thus be unacceptable to a régime based on the value of security. A debt restructure would effectively expropriate bond holders, inflation would eat away at savings, and a tax on wealth would – worst of all – demand particularly large contributions from the top 1 per cent, who own 27 per cent of the wealth; while barely affecting the bottom 50 per cent who own barely 22.7 per cent of the wealth, despite being 50 times more numerous than the top 1 per cent (World Inequality Database 2021). When 670,000 people at the top own more than 33.5 million people at the bottom, a tax on wealth would be unacceptable for a régime of the right.

Foreign policy and security

France's foreign policy is also a key component of Macron's security strategy and inscribes itself in a continuum of his ideology. The analysis of domestic politics, where open-society liberals are contrasted with closed-society nationalists, is replicated on the international stage, where struggles are conceptualized between the defenders of the liberal order and authoritarian régimes – notably China, Russia, and jihadist movements. This continuity was highlighted by Macron himself, in his preface to the armed forces strategic review of 2017 which he initiated at the beginning of his presidency. The security of the nation is framed as a collection of all national resources, at home and abroad, notably involving French businesses (Ministère des Armées 2017, 5–8). Unsurprisingly, France's power is considered not only in military terms, but also in terms of the economic resources it can muster, particularly when it comes from business interests and the soft power they confer. Playing on notions of soft and normative power, Macron has continued the foreign policy of the post-Cold War liberal order, where France privileges multilateral action, international institutions, notably the UN, and attempts to build European defence capacity.

At the European level first, Macron has pushed for a consolidation of Franco-German relations, based on his strategy of *en même temps*. At the same time, Macron has opted for both celebration of Franco-German cooperation, symbolically by celebrating the 100-year anniversary of the 1918 armistice with Angela Merkel at Rethondes, and confrontation, with a challenge to Berlin's resistance to financial integration at the European level during the COVID-19 pandemic. Continuing what his minister Clément Beaune (2020) insists are the two main trends of French foreign policy towards Berlin – celebration and confrontation – Macron's European strategy has been both to build on existing relations between Paris and Berlin, while also seeking alternatives where the agenda of both capitals clashed. By finding alliances with other EU members, Macron managed to convince Germany to make more funds available in 2020 to combat the pandemic, despite growing national debts in Europe and German reticence to expand credit beyond existing levels. In the end, more than €800 billion of funds were allocated in May 2020, on top of the Union's existing budget. This is significant not so much for the amount of money spent – it pales in comparison with the US stimulus in response to the virus – but rather because it empowered European institutions to borrow money directly on financial markets. At the same time as defending French sovereignty when it comes to its foreign policy, Macron has thus achieved EU sovereignty – to a limited extent – by strengthening EU institutions, and their ability to finance themselves. The outlook of these reforms is pro-business and favours change through technological novelty, with funds going towards climate and digital transition, research and innovation, recovery and resilience in the face of health threats, modernizing agricultural policy, fighting climate change, biodiversity protection, and gender equality. Few could argue against the need for investment in those areas – making these technical solutions to problems perceived to be technical. Macron's neutralization of politics from debates, his lack of focus on issues pertaining to the safety of Europeans in their everyday lives, and his technocratic politics is perhaps best suited for the EU level, where political disagreements are largely absent given the technical nature of many of the institutions.

This double talk, when it comes to sovereignty – both French and European – and when it comes to French–German cooperation, with Macron acting both with Germany and beyond its interests, is the liberal utopia Macron could only dream of prior to his election. Based on a type of normative power and political persuasion, it seeks the best of both worlds, where France is both independent and reaping the benefits of multilateral institutions. In a sense, it reflects the reality of French foreign policy – with a limited capacity for intervention and to project its power, it seeks innovative and ingenious ways to exert influence abroad to satisfy its interests. France's continued involvement in Mali, and the Sahel region more widely, is testament to French foreign policy ambitions and limitations. At one level, France was able to project power in Mali, Niger, Chad, Burkina Faso and Mauritania with little international help outside of African partners. Operation Barkhane, which started in 2014, was inherited by Macron from his predecessor, with the task of combatting terrorist groups and insurgents in the Sahel region, expanding the existing operation already in place in Mali (Majumdar 2020, 53). In his analysis of French intervention in Africa, Benedikt Erforth (2020) highlights the double nature of French military doctrine under Macron as a continuation of an attempt to bring forth a type of 'European interventionism', to use Macron's own words. Macron's dream of a *Europe de la défense*, however, was frustrated by the reluctance of European partners before 2022 to share his objectives for the creation of a European defence budget and strike force capable of rapid intervention. French unilateral intervention was thus the reluctant outcome of France's failure to convince partners to join its operations – although Paris continued to seek international partners once French boots were on the ground. The inclusion of small contingents of British, Estonian and Swedish troops in Operation Barkhane can be seen as evidence of France's continued attempts to widen its multilateral approach in Western Africa.

The French response to the Russian invasion of Ukraine in February 2022 has shaken European countries – but largely played to the strengths of Macron's international security strategy. Although the French President suffered a humiliating defeat when it came to his attempts to use soft power in the days that preceded the invasion, his call for higher military integration within the EU is now more palatable to many within the institution. Macron had visited his Russian and Ukrainian counterparts in February 2022, days before the outbreak of war, securing personal guarantees from the Kremlin that it had no plans for invasion. One can hardly blame Macron for attempting to broker a deal between the two parties ahead of hostilities, but the personal relationship between himself and Putin seemed stretched beyond repair following the betrayal of trust between the two presidents. Once again reflecting the limitations of French power, the hard reality seemed to be that Macron's influence over his Russian counterpart was almost nonexistent. In the weeks that followed the invasion, Macron was spearheading international efforts to sanction Russia, as well as supporting Ukraine, short of military involvement. Military equipment, including weapons, was quickly sent to support the Ukrainian armed forces. It was on the diplomatic scene, however, that Macron particularly shined. After he had called for higher EU cooperation on defence, renewed Russian aggression in Eastern Europe brought previously recalcitrant EU countries to Macron's side. Germany, notably, dramatically changed its stance on rearmament, with €100 billion of new spending announced by the Scholz government within days of the Russian advance into Ukraine, with the potential to outpace France's budget as a percentage of GDP in the near future. Macron, of course, has also announced a rise in military budgets, further contributing to the security shift of his presidency and continuing the rise in military spending started in 2019.

The French approach to international security – multilateral when possible, unilateral when needed – has raised particular issues internally in France under Macron's presidency. Already dissatisfied with the status quo in 2017, military forces in France have become increasingly vocal about their political position. Overstretched by their deployment in operations abroad as well as a continued anti-terror role at home, French armed forces have continually asked for better means to fulfil their missions. Stagnant in the first two years of Macron's presidency, the military budget has risen since 2019, with further plans for a rapid expansion of expenditure in this area by 2025 (Vincent 2021). The Macron régime is slowing giving itself the means to enforce its international security policy, and one can expect a growing assertiveness of French interventionism if current projects materialize. Macron's willingness to join military operations in Syria and Libya, in addition to existing commitments in Western Africa, could be concrete signs of the rhetoric of liberal interventionism he has been keen to defend.

In 2021, two open letters were published by former and current members of the armed forces, denouncing laxity on the part of the government. Identifying three harms, the 20 retired generals who signed the first of these letters denounced antiracism, Islamism, and use of excessive force against demonstrators – particularly against the *gilets jaunes* – justifying their public outcry (Fabre-Bernadac 2021). In the second letter, signed by active members of the armed forces, these themes are repeated, with the added thinly veiled threat that the army is ready to intervene in the case of a civil war in France (Valeurs Actuelles 2021). Although the threat of a civil war in France may seem far-fetched, these interventions point to two important conclusions about the state of the French armed forces. They see themselves as overstretched, with the security ambitions of the French state not matched by the means provided to them. In addition, they perceive their mission to fight terrorism and extremism abroad as being at odds with internal security policies – and their role on French soil. Citing the example of insecurity in the *banlieues*, where 'Islamism and suburban hordes' defy the Republic, they question if the French state is truly committed to combatting extremism and terrorism, given its perceived laxity towards homegrown variants of these phenomena. Instead, they see that they are deployed to deter protesters at home – as was the case in 2019 when Macron deployed military forces around key monuments in Paris at the height of the *gilets jaunes* protests. A form of identity politics is clearly at play here: while many members of the armed forces would have sympathized with the *gilets jaunes* protesters, few could identify with the plight of the *banlieues* (Poncet 2019). The right-wing polemicist Éric Zemmour claimed, in 2016, to have sources in the armed forces saying they were training for military intervention in the *banlieues*. Although the credibility of these sources is unknown, the spectre of military forces intervening has been raised numerous times in French political discourse, notably under Sarkozy, and more recently in 2020 by Macron's interior minister, Christophe Castaner, who dismissed that solution not on principle, but because it would risk an escalation of violence (Leboucq 2021). The separation between internal security and exterior security is still permeable in France, where military presence on French soil has been a common feature of everyday life since the creation of the Plan Vigipirate in 1978 that created the mechanism for the army's role in counterterrorist action at home.

Conclusion

The security state is not an unfortunate consequence of neoliberal ideology, as identified in Macron's presidency. It is a necessary part of the vision of society promoted by this ideology: just as the expansion of the state's influence is necessary to expand markets, the securitization of populations is necessary to fulfil the social vision of the Macron régime. Foucault has given us important tools to understand this rise of security in the contemporary period, with consequences for understanding Macron's policies and ideas. Security is an essential value for those on the right of the political spectrum, with a particular emphasis being placed on the safeguarding of property and property relations. A particular securitization of the population is at play, with the deployment of technologies of power to keep control over the population as a whole. We have seen that this focus on security is not inevitable or necessary: the notion of *sûreté*, defined as safety and certainty, can provide a sense of solidarity in a modern economic context. The response to the COVID-19 pandemic shows that another economic model is possible, one where safety for all and certainty about economic relations is made a priority of the state. Measures pertaining to *sûreté* had historically been introduced by parties of the right, effectively widening solidarity at the national level, up to the 1970s. Since the 1980s, both left and right parties in power in France have presided over a relative decline of the welfare state, with the speed and state of that decline more or less pronounced depending on circumstances and political will. What we have seen in France since 2017 is a rapid pace of change, to effectively make the remaining features of the welfare state dependent on the securitization of property relations. We recall the analysis made in Chapter 1 of Macron's welfare state reforms: reforms in labour law, unemployment insurance, and pensions. The focus on security rather than safety demands far less generous, far more uncertain, and far cheaper social welfare programmes. If it had not been for the COVID-19 pandemic, Macron's ideal of security would not have shown its alternative colours, would not have shown that the securitization of the state is not inevitable, would have obfuscated the need for more than just security in the need for certainty and safety.

3

Merit

'I prefer the Republic's exams, they're meritocratic', said Macron in 2016 in relation to his alma mater, the ENA (Pedder 2018, 77). Macron is fond of equality. It is a feature of his programme, put together in his autobiographical work *Révolution* (Macron, 2016), as well as a recurrent theme in his speeches and addresses to the nation. For those who maintain that Macron is a politician of both left and right, equality is the value that underpins his pragmatism and his desire for social justice. It is indubitable that equality plays an important part in Macron's ideology, but the argument I put forward in this chapter is that it is a very specific type of equality that Macron defends, an equality in the face of luck, an equality against discrimination, and an equality of opportunity. This type of equality is better described as merit – the desert and worth of a particular individual independently of circumstances around them. This makes Macron sensitive to specific types of inequalities (those due to race and gender, for example), but also puts together a particular vision of the individual as someone responsible for their own fate – and ultimately their own failures and experience of the vicissitudes of life. In the first instance, I will show that Macron's liberal-libertarian compromise is the blending of two types of liberalism found in Rawls and Nozick. I then move on to show that it is in the philosophy of Dworkin that this attitude towards equality comes together in a form of 'luck egalitarianism', which is the culmination of Macron's thought on equality. This lays open the question of the vision of the individual developed by Macron, and its roots in a very specific, responsibility-driven conception of the person with specific theological roots. For this, we will turn to Weber's seminal work on the Protestant ethic and the concepts of grace and the calling. A secularized version of these concepts is central to Macron's ideology, although their roots in particular conception of Christianity cannot be avoided altogether. I then show that this secularized political theology can be understood alongside what Sandel defines as 'the meritocracy', before providing a critique of the notion of responsibility using Nietzsche. Finally, I conclude this chapter with a brief exploration of the technocratic nature of Macron's rule, which is the institutionalized version of the value of merit and forms his preferred style of rule.

The liberal-libertarian compromise

While discussing the crisis of the *gilets jaunes* in another book, I argued that Macron's policies in the first two years of his mandate were those of a liberal-libertarian compromise (Devellennes 2021). Let me quickly recount what I said then, so that we can build on this analysis for the present question of Macron's ideology. For Rawls, the theory of justice revolves around a double purpose. In the first instance, it is meant to justify inequalities, and in the second instance, it is meant to justify redistribution of resources for the least advantaged members of society. Without going into much more detail, the Rawlsian compromise is that inequalities are justified only inasmuch as they improve the conditions of those at the bottom, which at least theoretically allows for large (and growing) inequalities in wealth, as long those at the bottom see at least *some* improvement in their material conditions. We know that Macron was influenced by Rawls, and that his team of advisers are fans of the US television series *The West Wing*, which is still one of the best defences of a Rawlsian perspective in popular culture (Plowright 2017, 174). A scene from the show helps to illustrate this Rawlsian idealism. Sam Seaborn, a White House staffer in the fictional Democratic administration of the George W. Bush years, lectures union leaders, explaining:

> 'I left Gage Whitney making $400,000 a year, which means I paid twenty-seven times the national average in income tax. I paid my fair share, and the fair share of twenty-six other people. And I'm happy to because that's the only way it's gonna work, and it's in my best interest that everybody be able to go to schools and drive on roads, but I don't get twenty-seven votes on Election Day.' (Sorkin et al 2006, Season 2, Episode 20)

In this scenario, the highly successful lawyer-turned-adviser-to-the-President illustrates the Rawlsian attitude to redistribution: everyone benefits from public infrastructure and spending, justifying a progressive taxation system. But the system also guarantees equal political rights, and here there is a tension between the sense of entitlement felt by Seaborn and the political reality of the democratic process. In Rawls' terms, the property rights of all are guaranteed under the first principle of justice (equal liberties for all), alongside political rights such as the right to vote, and only then does the difference principle come into play, justifying redistribution. As Sam Seaborn concludes his argument: "The top one percent of wage earners in this country pay for twenty-two percent of this country. Let's not call them names while they're doing it, is all I'm saying" (Sorkin 2006, Season 2, Episode 20).

Robert Nozick, a colleague of Rawls at Harvard University, fundamentally disagreed with the basis of the theory of justice. Arguing from a libertarian perspective, he proposed that inequalities are always just as long as the acquisition of property was just. In other words, if one enters a contractual agreement with another, and benefits greatly from the freely entered contract, the wealth acquisition that derives from it is fully justified. Any redistribution, as Nozick famously argued, 'is on a par with forced labor' (Nozick 2001, 169) since it is the equivalent of forcing an individual to work part of the time for others' benefit. The corollary to this position is that even if taxes are justified to make a minimal state work, any type of redistribution such as progressive taxation is unjust. It is a popular position, notably in the United States, but also in France where public taxation is often a large burden on independent and small businesses. Although the label '*libertaire*' has a different connotation in French, often closer to communist and anarchist movements, Nozick's utopia is not without support from the liberal right. Macron's flagship fiscal measure, the suppression of the ISF, expresses this sentiment well. Those who have acquired large wealth (over €1.3 million) should not be taxed on their success, as such wealth was legitimately acquired – and taxes have already been paid on their income. But perhaps more telling was the flat tax on revenues from capital introduced by Macron. Less publicized, as the income from dividends does not tax work but rather affects accumulated capital, it nevertheless marked the trajectory of Macron's presidency. It effectively introduced a regressive taxation system, where top-bracket earners with no capital would pay 45 per cent tax on their income from work, while the very richest in society, who earn their income almost exclusively from dividends, would see their tax rate drop to 30 per cent. Simultaneously, Macron's government reduced the top bracket of corporate tax from 33 per cent in 2017 to 25 per cent in 2022, thereby enlarging the proportion of profits to be shared with shareholders or reinvested in capital. We thus see a liberal-libertarian compromise in Macron's rule: the bottom 50 per cent see wealth redistribution that comes from the top 50 per cent, but among the top bracket the wealthiest 10 per cent of individuals (the upper class) contribute less than the 40 per cent below them (the middle classes). In short: there is redistribution between the middle and lower classes, but a more libertarian model for the upper classes, becoming even more acute as we reach the top 1 per cent or even 0.1 per cent of the population. This is what I have called the liberal-libertarian compromise: a mixture of a progressive model of redistribution with a regressive form of taxation at the very top.

Brute luck and option luck

Macron's own ideology on equality is inspired by the philosophy of Ronald Dworkin, as he himself confirmed in an interview with Sophie Pedder (2018, 152). In two essays published in 1981, Dworkin argued against what he calls 'equality of welfare' and in favour of an 'equality of resources'. At the root of his critique of equality of welfare lies a distinction between two types of luck: option luck and brute luck; hence he is thought to be the founder of a school of thought named 'luck egalitarianism'. Let us deal with these two distinctions in turn. In the first instance, we may consider what Dworkin means by equality of welfare. For Dworkin (1981a, 189), the concept of welfare is used 'to describe what is fundamental in life rather than what is instrumental'. Dworkin (1981a, 190) argues that this distinction, between fundamental and instrumental needs in life is insufficient because we cannot always tell whether differences between two individuals are due to 'the cost of their tastes or in the adequacy of their physical or mental powers'. In other words, if an individual such as Macron has developed a taste for Corton white wine from Burgundy (Femme Actuelle 2020), it may be because he has acquired a delicate palate sensitive to the subtle aroma of this particular *vignoble*, which sells for around €100 a bottle. If another individual gets the same welfare, or fulfilment of fundamental needs, from drinking a *vin de table*, at less than €3 a bottle, then the welfare theory of equality could be said to favour the redistribution of resources towards those with fine taste, for whom consuming the cheaper option would occasion intense displeasure. Dworkin's point is thus that the welfare theory is inadequate, as it cannot convincingly argue that one person's welfare is the same as another, and thus leads to absurd demands for redistribution that favour not the least advantaged, as Rawls had wished, but the most advantaged.

On the other hand, an equality of resources bypasses, according to Dworkin (1981b, 297), the difficulties raised by the welfarist model. He argues, this time more in response to Nozick than to Rawls, that we should favour an initially equal distribution of material resources, complemented by two hypothetical insurance markets: one for talent and one for handicap. The situation described by Dworkin is, of course, abstract, supposing that all individuals have equal resources to start with and use these resources to buy hypothetical insurance against the natural inequalities of life. Each decides, a priori, the level of risk acceptable to them, and they are left with more or fewer resources depending on how far they buy in to the insurance scheme. This hypothetical situation of equality functions as a free market of talents and accidents, where all are responsible for their own level of luck since they choose to buy, or not to buy, insurance in the first place. The central message of Dworkin is that outcomes cannot be equalized, but initial resources can – at least theoretically. It relies on a market of resource allocation, deemed to be fair because it compensates for the accidents of life. Macron's own philosophy follows this logic closely. Fairness is not about redistribution through welfare, but rather about creating conditions as if citizens were given access to similar resources. As Macron told Pedder in an interview in 2017, 'Some will do well, others less so. But I will protect you from the great accidents of life and I will help give you the capacity to succeed' (Pedden 2018, 153). The vision of the state as a great insurer, rather than as a system of welfare provision, dominates the thinking of the President. As Dworkin was writing his theory of equality, the welfare state was coming under increasing pressure – the premiership of Thatcher and presidency of Reagan, as well as the liberal turn of the Socialist Party in France under Mitterrand, all testify to this trend. The attack on welfare, on the grounds that it could favour those who do not need it, has been difficult to root out of political thinking ever since. When Macron declared that France was spending 'crazy dough' on its welfare system (Colin 2018), he was embracing the anti-welfare sentiment, with welfare to be replaced by the justice of an ideal market of insurances that exists nowhere: a market utopia such as the one we find in Dworkin.

Dworkin's utopia is based on a notion of personal responsibility that is at the core of the thinking behind the anti-welfare liberalism also espoused by Macron. For Dworkin, this is based on a distinction between brute luck and option luck. 'Option luck is a matter of how deliberate and calculated gambles turn out—whether someone gains or loses through accepting an isolated risk he or she should have anticipated and might have declined. Brute luck is how risks fall out that are not in that sense deliberate gambles' (Dworkin 2000). Brute luck, for an egalitarian like Dworkin, needs to be equalized. Option luck, on the other hand, requires no such equalization. If someone is born with a particular disability, they deserve the equalization of their condition. If, on the other hand, someone is born with talents but squanders them through bad choices of their own, then no such equalization is possible. Under Dworkin's scheme, only accidents wholly outside of an individual's control deserve measures of equality. If someone takes a gamble, and fails, they are left without help or resources to bring themselves back up. But equally, if someone is particularly unlucky in terms of social status and/or genetic inheritance, they deserve help to bring themselves up in a society where they have suffered a clear disadvantage through no fault of their own. There is an intuitive appeal to Dworkin's theory: those who have squandered their talent deserve no public help, while those who face obstacles through sheer lack of luck deserve public support. Choice and fault, as Arneson puts it in his description of Dworkin's thought, 'are combined in the idea of option luck' (Arneson 2018, 58). Macron's rhetoric, as well as his policies, have matched this Dworkinian ideal. When the President told a 25-year-old man called Jonathan who was explaining to Macron that he could not find work in the horticulture sector to 'cross the road' to find work, he was clearly alluding to the young man's self-inflicted unemployment (Le Parisien 2018). Telling the young man to go work in a café or a restaurant, when that young man was exhibiting his distress at not being able to find vocational work, shows the emphasis placed on personal responsibility for economic distress. The following year, in 2019, Macron's government reduced unemployment insurance to save €4.5 billion during the presidential term. This anecdote and that policy change show the overall trend of the régime: unemployment is conceived as a result of option luck, not brute luck. If a person cannot find a job in their preferred field, they have to go where employment is available. This particular attitude to employment was made obsolete during the response to COVID-19, and reforms to the unemployment benefits had to be pushed back. Precisely because the outbreak of the disease was in no way conceivable as the responsibility of the French population, because it was brute luck rather than option luck, Macron had to use the power available to the state to remedy the situation. Unlike with unemployment, as we shall see below, the inability to work during COVID-19 lockdowns merited state involvement and aid, which were made readily available by the French government. Far from being an exception to the régime's conception of individual responsibility, the response to the pandemic illustrated its attitude towards merit and desert.

The calling and grace

The notion of individual responsibility is at the core of the Macron régime. It has its roots in what Max Weber defined, in his seminal essay of the same name, as the *spirit of capitalism*. Weber's analysis is based on a careful consideration of the religious roots of the ethics of Western capitalism. The rise of an ethic where 'the earning of more and more money, combined with the strict avoidance of all spontaneous enjoyment of life ... appears entirely transcendental and absolutely irrational' (Weber 2005, 18), because it is based on theological concepts that have since been secularized. Weber provides a classic example of political theology: how a modern conception of the public good has roots in older religious traditions, through an analysis of two values that emerge and become dominant during the Protestant reformation: the *calling* (*Beruf* in German, sometimes translated as 'vocation'), and *grace*. Let us take these in turn.

It is with Luther's conception of the calling that this political theology begins. Although the notion had existed before the Reformation, and rests on a reading and translating of the Bible by Luther, its modern significance only arises in the modern era. It takes the form of 'the valuation of the fulfilment of duty in worldly affairs as the highest form which the moral activity of the individual could assume' (Weber 2005, 40). The everyday thus acquires religious significance, in a way in which this was not true in Medieval Catholic theology. Against the ascetic monasticism of Catholic orders, the Protestant churches gradually established themselves as the defenders of a radically different ethic, no longer based on the renouncement of material worldly goods, but rather in a new form of asceticism that put the duty of fulfilling one's calling, of partaking in worldly labour activity, as the primary means to glorify God. Of course, one need not accept the particular theology of Luther to accept that the notion of calling, secularized after the Reformation during the modern era, has taken a particular transcendental significance. This was already Weber's point, as what makes the theological concept political is precisely its ability to translate into non-religious terms and affect change in public settings outside of the religious community.

In Macron's *Révolution*, we find such a secularized concept of the calling. His family's *ascension* – the term evokes already a certain transcendence – from modest origins to the provincial bourgeoisie, occurred through knowledge (*savoir*) (Macron 2016, 12). His personal trajectory, he claims, reflected this family path, and he had to work hard to achieve it. He discusses his *conviction* – again, the term evokes a religious root – that 'nothing is more precious than the free disposition of one's person, the pursuit of a self-selected project, the realization of one's talent, what ever it is' (Macron 2016, 12). This conviction – one might say, calling – brought him to politics, once a career in the literary field was made unlikely by his failed application to the ENS. He thus studied – by conviction – philosophy at Nanterre, and politics 'by the greatest of coincidences [*par le plus grand des hasards*],' brought him to Sciences Po Paris (Macron 2016, 19). It is a sense of calling, in the Weberian sense invoked above, that drove Macron into politics. His calling could have been otherwise – he was interested in literature and philosophy, and wrote unpublished novels – but his duty called him elsewhere, combining his interest in philosophy with a training at France's most elite political science universities: the Institut d'Études Politiques de Paris, and then eventually to ENA. Notwithstanding the fact that there is no *hasard*, no coincidence about entering Sciences Po, whose selection process through a strenuous *concours*, or competitive exam, is highly selective, Macron's recollection of his calling is telling of his acceptance of the Weberian notion itself. Macron could have been a great scholar of French literature, a renowned philosopher, or a successful author of great novels. But his calling was elsewhere. He worked tirelessly at Sciences Po, at ENA, in the French administration, at the Rothschild Bank, as a minister, as a political entrepreneur and finally as President of the Republic, to answer this calling. As Weber notes, there is something transcendental and irrational about this attitude. But it is perfectly understandable as a calling, as a vocation and devotion to a higher cause. This higher cause, for Macron, is, of course, not God. It is a vision for France, a political project. The calling is secularized, but it emphasizes the need for engagement with the world and fulfilment of one's potential, and a notion of mission which cannot be explained in purely instrumental terms.

If the calling in Luther's theology makes participation in worldly activity a religious duty, it is in Calvin's theological notion of *grace* that the spirit of capitalism finds its final formulation. Although the notion of grace had importance before Calvin, it took on a particular meaning in the theologian's work through the doctrine of predestination. God's grace, in Calvinism, is given by God to the select few. Those who are not predestined for His grace either receive His mercy or not, and the wicked and ungodly will be judged by God (Weber 2005, 58–9). But the predestined few, those with God's grace, have the power and knowledge to do good. There is thus a tension between the notion of grace, predestined by God's choice as to whom to confer it upon, and the effects of grace, which enable the select few to do good in the world. It is not that one's grace is determined by good actions in the world – in line with one's calling – but that the chosen ones are able to do good in the world through some divine spark within them. As Weber notes, this is a break with a more magical tradition, whereby one might hope to attain God's grace. In Calvinism, grace is either granted or not; there is nothing one can do in the world that can change it. For Weber, however, it was not satisfactory merely to have faith that one is among those endowed with God's grace, as Calvin had argued, and predestination in the Calvinist Church soon mutated due to the demands of pastoral work (Weber 2005, 66). Faith alone was not enough to believe that one is chosen by God, hence 'in order to attain that self-confidence intense worldly activity is recommended as the most suitable means. It and it alone disperses religious doubts and gives the certainty of grace' (Weber 2005, 67). Although the Church never abandoned predestination fully, it mutated it into a form that is more suitable to being preached. One is either chosen by God or one is not; one either has grace or one does not. But one's certitude that one is chosen can be fostered by worldly activity – intense and successful. Only this success in one's worldly calling will give the believer certainty that one is chosen (even though this grace is still predetermined). The Calvinist, in a sense, does not create their own salvation but rather creates their certainty of it (Weber 2005, 69–70). If someone wastes their talents, it is a sure sign that they are not chosen by God. But if someone is successful and fulfils their talents, it is merely a sign that they can be sure – as much as one can be sure of something which involves an act of faith – that God has chosen them and anointed them with grace. It is thus a lifetime project to convince oneself that one truly has been chosen by God. It requires method and dedication, hard work but also success. Anyone who does not meet these criteria is not one of the select few, and merits, at best, mercy and, in any case, judgement. Coming back to the case of Jonathan, the young unemployed man mentioned above who had failed to find a career in horticulture, we see how the notions of calling and grace come together in the spirit of capitalism. Although he had thought his calling was in that particular field, he clearly did not have the grace necessary to make it in that field. Interviewed a year after the encounter with Macron, Jonathan describes having worked in the seasonal catering industry over the summer in Brittany. Graceless, but not having forgotten his calling, he explains he is still applying for jobs working with plants (Bourgeois and Vichard, 2019).

Macron himself has come from a meritocratic model within which he has been highly successful. But this is not enough to infer that he has embraced a notion of grace, even if in a secularized manner. For evidence of this belief, one needs to turn to Macron's rhetoric. Labelled *macronades* by commentators, even before he was elected president, Macron's outbursts have revealed much about his inner thoughts. While inaugurating Station F in 2017, a start-up campus in the middle of Paris, Macron commented that the building is situated in an old railway station, a place where 'people who succeed and people who are nothing' meet (Le Scan Politique 2017). The successful and those who are nothing closely resembles a secularized version of the Calvinist doctrine of grace described earlier, between those chosen by God and those who merely deserve His mercy. In addition to echoing the notion of those who are chosen and those who are not, the comment came as a warning to the young entrepreneurs he was addressing on the new campus. It was a warning that success in their investment was not everything. That even if they are successful in their endeavours, they have to remember that they started in this place, that they benefited from the opportunities given to them, and that they have a duty towards those 'who are nothing'. In other terms, although certainly the phrasing came across as a public relations blunder, it was reflective of a broader position which Macron defends more deeply. Those who succeed in one single endeavour are not the elected few. They are not those with secular grace. Only those who have succeeded but continued their mission and fulfilled their vocation through a lifetime of business success are those who can be sure of their own secular salvation. 'Never forget,' Macron continued, with reference to these entrepreneurs' capacity to change their own country, 'that you have a duty to make changes in the long run, that at each moment this responsibility that comes from having been born or raised in this railway station, in Paris, in France, in Europe, somewhere in the world, and that you will bear [this responsibility] with you throughout your life.' This is the sense in which Macron's grace is a secularized version of Calvin's grace. It shares the sense that some are elected while others are nothing; it shares the sense that grace enables some individuals to succeed in life where others do not; it shares the sense that only a continual life of worldly duties, and a constant sense of responsibility to fulfil one's calling brings the individual closer to the conviction that they are, indeed, chosen for a higher purpose. The select few are opposed, as Macron commented in a discourse in Athens, to those who resist his revolution and reforms, 'the lazy, cynics, and extremists' (Le Point 2017). The lazy, of course, cannot demonstrate their grace, while the cynics and extremists are those who do not have faith in the project. Macron's conviction, of his own calling as a revolutionary setting out his vision of what France needs to be, is nothing short of religious. Those without faith in the project endanger the republic *per se*. They are extremists, apostates of the progressive church which Macron promises as a means of salvation.

Meritocracy

In the context of increasing inequalities, with levels of inequality rising closer to those of the *Belle Époque*, when they were at their highest, the doctrines of calling and grace come together to justify a meritocratic system. This is, of course, not only a French phenomenon, and has repercussions worldwide. In an unequal society, Sandel notes in the US context, 'those who land on top want to believe their success is morally justified, […] that] they have earned their success through their own talent and hard work (Sandel 2020, 13). Where there are failures to the meritocratic story – where merit is not the primary reason for a person's success, for example – the failure is attributed to the remnants of the old régime, a system imperfectly meritocratic. But, as Sandel argues, the issue is not whether or how to perfect the meritocratic model, but rather that there are flaws inherent in the model itself, as a moral ideal to analyze society. Even in an ideal meritocratic society, where all advantages in life can be attributed back to one's own merit, and where winners and losers are perfectly aligned with their individual merit, such a utopia would breed unattractive attitudes, according to Sandel: 'Among the winners, it generates hubris; among the losers, humiliation and resentment' (Sandel 2020, 25).

This double consequence of our contemporary meritocracy – hubris and resentment – is at the centre of the problem of technocratic politics. In France, the technocratic meritocratic ideal which breeds hubris and resentment is most evident in the crisis of the *gilets jaunes* and the Macron régime's response to it. I have covered this at length elsewhere, so let me just recap one example here. When Edouard Philippe's government reduced speed limits on French national roads to 80 kilometres an hour, and announced a new tax on fuel, he was doing what every good technocrat would do. In an era of global warming, deadly road accidents, and financial strain, the measures promised a win-win outcome for the French government. They would reduce carbon emissions by disincentivizing motorized travel, they would reduce accidents through the new reduced speed, and they would strengthen the public purse, by raising money badly needed to meet the government's target of balancing budgets. This was without counting on the determination of those who need their cars to go to work, take their children to school, and do their weekly errands – the residents of peripheral France – to fight those measures. What started as a protest movement against specific technocratic measures soon escalated, however, to a channelling of much deeper resentment against the technocratic classes, based in the metropoles, making decisions for the periphery. The clash between the hubris of the government – Philippe refused to reconsider the measures, until he had no other choice, as Macron and Philippe, after all, had the expert advice needed to make those technical decisions – and the *gilets jaunes* themselves, whose demands quickly centred around calling for the resignation of President Macron – illustrates the hubris/resentment dichotomy well.

The hubris of the technocratic class is evident in the rise of credentialism: the prejudice that university-level education is necessary for higher office, or even makes one individual better than others, and that education is the answer to inequality. As Sandel notes, it is one of the last accepted prejudices that elites flaunt openly. Attitudes to other disfavoured groups pale in comparison to elites' attitude to those without a college degree, and elites are 'unembarrassed by their prejudice' (Sandel 2020, 95–6). People without a college degree are virtually absent from elected office, in sharp contrast to the situation half a century ago. According to Sandel, one can attribute the work-friendly policies of the New Deal, in the US, and of the Attlee government, in the UK, to their wide inclusion of non-university graduates to their ranks. Seven of Attlee's ministers, he notes, had worked as coal miners (Sandel 2020, 100). As Macron rose to power, he surrounded himself with the *Macron boys* (the English-language phrase is used in French), a group of advisers coming from the elite schools at the top of the French higher education system. These advisers, highly skilled technocrats with the highest qualifications available in France, proposed a frictionless and neutral politics. We have already seen in Chapter 2 that this neutral politics in fact always already incorporates practices of neutralization when in power. Attempts to enforce purely technocratic measures depend on a particular security apparatus, with a growing role for law enforcement forces to violently push through the new rules of the game.

Michael Sandel proposes an alternative to the tyranny of merit he paints such an eloquent picture of. His alternative is based on recognizing work. The principle of recognition is important because it goes beyond the purely economic aspects of workers' place in society, to rework their status as producers (Sandel 2020, 208). Based on the theory of recognition found in Hegel, and articulated by Honneth (1992), Sandel makes the point that the labour market is a system for recognition. 'It not only remunerates work with an income but publicly recognizes each person's work as a contribution to the common good' (Sandel 2020, 211). What this means in practice is open to debate and articulation, but Sandel proposes shifting the burden of taxation from work to consumption and speculation. Instead of payroll taxes, he proposes consumption, wealth and financial taxes. This is very much in line with Piketty's analysis, in that he proposes to introduce a tax on wealth that is properly progressive. Instead, as we have seen, the Macron régime has reinforced tax inequalities by moving towards increasingly regressive taxation systems, especially at the very top. Sandel's vision of fairness is based around replacing the current hubris of the elites with a sense of humility. If billionaires are not entirely responsible for their own success, if they have benefited from luck and social help, a favourable climate for investment and the work of their employees, they should contribute much more than they currently do. But Sandel is missing a step here. We must first demonstrate why the ethic of responsibility, which emerged from the Protestant ethic, and of the value it attaches to the calling and to grace, came about.

Responsibility

The flip side of merit is responsibility. If those who succeed merit the rewards of their hard work and success, then those who do not succeed are also responsible for their own failures. The *macronades*, Macron's tirades uttered towards ordinary citizens, point to this measure of success and failure. If one only has to cross the street to find work, if employees facing redundancy are considered illiterate, if the best way to afford a suit is to work, it points to the failure of those who have chosen a career where jobs are sparse, those with insufficient levels of education, and those who are out of work. Nietzsche had diagnosed this importance of the ethic of responsibility in a much more critical way than Weber did, as a symptom of a wider sociocultural ethic running deep in the Western psyche.

For Nietzsche, our belief in responsibility is rooted in the theological concept of the freedom of the will. Free will, he claims, is the root of our belief in individual responsibility, which is otherwise incompatible with human beings' determinateness. Scientific inquiry suggests that humans are determined by social, cultural, accidental, circumstantial, psychological and other factors entirely outside of their control, but yet we cling on to the notion of individual responsibility as a key feature of our humanity (Nietzsche 2001, 21). The reason for this is that we hold on to the belief that we are the cause of ourselves, the *causa sui* that is the origin of our other choices in life. This concept of *causa sui,* for Nietzsche (2001, 16), 'is something thoroughly absurd' that nevertheless holds a profound influence on Christian societies in particular. Based around the mythology of the Fall, where humanity has been made responsible for its own demise and exclusion from the idyllic garden of Eden, the notion of free will has been central to the development of notions of responsibility in the Christian world. If free will has been refuted a hundred times, as Nietzsche (2001, 18) claims, what explains its persistence in the secularized world that followed the decline in

Christianity's influence as an organized religion? It could be that it is simply a convenient shorthand for articulating notions of responsibility – which may be required for social order and political agency. Let us take an example from Macron's response to the issue of unemployment before we come back to Nietzsche's critique of free will in more detail.

In *Révolution*, Macron (2016, 69) argues for a two-pronged approach to tackle unemployment. In the first instance, more opportunities have to be created for the 'victims' of the current system – the youth, the least educated, naturalized citizens, future generations, those on short-term contracts, single-parent families and those unable to find adequate housing. Without a rethinking of the current system, Macron warned, this army of victims will grow, crushing hope for a better France. We will come back to the recreation of hope in Chapter 4 but let us focus here on what these victims have in common. They are not responsible for their own fate. What the presidential candidate promised was a world of opportunities, where those with a will to succeed can achieve their goals. The enemy of such a dream, and the second step of the approach to unemployment, is to curb public spending. To 'give all the same chances and the same opportunities', Macron (2016, 71) continues, we have to get rid of corporatist protections and offer new social protections that give all rights, but also impose duties. These duties are framed in terms of a responsibility for individuals to create, to move, and to *entreprendre* (Macron 2016, 74) – all intransitive verbs to highlight that unemployment is a choice which can be remedied by a more entrepreneurial spirit. In terms of policies, these ideals have been translated into a thinning down of state guarantees against unemployment, and investment in key sectors judged to be at the spearhead of innovation. Bureaucratic rules around unemployment benefits were notably strengthened, lowering benefits received as well as restricting the right to those benefits further for those in long-term unemployment. Although some of these measures introduced in 2019 were put on hold due to the outbreak of the COVID-19 pandemic, they went ahead in 2021. Keeping with his pre-electoral promise, Macron also limited unemployment benefits further for managers [*cadres*], restricting benefits for those earning more than €4,500 per month (Droit-finances. net 2021). Consistent with an ethic of responsibility, Macron has shrunk public spending where those benefiting from state aid are perceived to be unreasonably picky about employment opportunities. Macron's strategy may well have worked in terms of reducing unemployment overall – unemployment fell from over 9 per cent in 2017 to almost 7 per cent in 2020, before shooting back up and stabilizing at 8 per cent in 2021 – but long-term unemployment is on the rise, with those seeking work for over a year growing in numbers (Insee 2021). An unsurprising consequence of the ethic of responsibility is the sidelining of those most vulnerable and at the margins of employment. Among those most affected by long-term unemployment are those who accept work to make ends meet but are on a long-term quest for employment in their profession of choice, and those with few qualifications who find it difficult to get a foothold in the labour market (Centre d'observation de la société 2020). A focus on individual responsibility can only go so far to explain what may otherwise be structural issues with the economy.

If Macron's political theology is anchored in a notion of responsibility that presupposes free will, it has strong repercussions for the way in which his administration treats French citizens. Note that here I do not argue that individuals bear no responsibility for their actions. Laws exist in France, as in other parliamentary democracies, to protect law and order. When an individual breaks the law – say, by burning a car or physically assaulting a police officer – they are legally responsible for their actions and must face the consequences. It is another step altogether, however, to perceive individuals as having free will, determining themselves and being ultimately responsible for their lives and all of the situations they face. Without doing away with the legal system altogether, it is reasonable to point out that part of the role of politics is to make informed decisions at the social level that precisely take individual's choices as being determined by factors outside their control. When it comes to youth unemployment, a lack of opportunities in rural or peripheral areas, or declining standards of living over prolonged periods of time – all social and economic realities in France under Macron's presidency – individuals are not free to determine their circumstances any more than they can choose their family background, skin colour or sexual preferences. While a lack of free will may have some consequences for our legal and penal practices, one need not throw the baby of law and order out with the bathwater of free will. Laws that deter crimes have a utility whether or not individuals are ultimately responsible for their own circumstances, and punishment for breaking the law can be thought of in terms that mediate and take into account the circumstances that led to crime being committed in the first place.

There is a false dichotomy, in other words, between free will and unfree will. One need not concede that a lack of free will means that individuals are ultimately unfree and make no relevant choices about themselves. Nietzsche argues precisely this fine line between free and unfree will. For him, the denial of free will also needs the denial of unfree will – if we are not ultimately responsible for who we are, we are nevertheless neither passive nor entirely determined by circumstances outside of our control. The balance, for Nietzsche, is in a clash of wills. Free will, argues Nietzsche, is the tool of the strong, who want to make those who have not been successful in life responsible for their own misery; but unfree will is the tool of the weak, who do not want to be responsible for anything and shift the blame onto someone else (Nietzsche 2001, 22). To put it in political terms, the liberal defends free will, while the socialist defends unfree will. But for Nietzsche, neither are correct in that it is precisely the clash of wills – of those who want to shift the blame onto others – that is the important conclusion of the analysis. If neither free nor unfree will are believable, we are left with a political struggle, an agonistic battle between levels of responsibility and the role that social forces play in that struggle. One can go beyond Nietzsche here and see that the issue of responsibility is precisely a political one – not a theological one. What can be done to alleviate circumstances that lead to socially undesirable outcomes is a much more fundamental question than who is responsible for those circumstances. The trouble with focusing on responsibility – whether it is Macron's political theology based on free will, or Nietzsche's socialist who believes in unfree will – is that it denies political agency altogether. For Macron, the solution to the problem of individual responsibility is technical rather than political. It relies on a technocratic vision of government agency, where experts are best placed to make decisions rather than solutions being of a political nature. The meritocracy he embodies relies on straightforward attribution of responsibility: the lazy unemployed versus the virtuous entrepreneurs. The solution is to create a climate that is favourable to the latter and hostile to the former. Never mind that such a vision is profoundly anchored in a vision of society that is itself entirely political – it portrays itself as anti-political, centrist, and neutral-technocratic.

Conclusion

Macron is the embodiment of the technocratic order *par excellence*. A graduate of the elite ENA, a civil servant and minister, as well as briefly a partner in a large bank, he has the credentials, competence and expertise characteristic of the technocratic class. As Christopher Bickerton and Carlo Invernizzi Accetti have noted, however, Macron is not only a representative of the technocratic class, but the archetype of a particular type of technopopulism: 'technopopulism through the leader' (Bickerton and Invernizzi Accetti 2021, 68). Bickerton and Invernizzi Accetti's thesis is that the two aspects of technocratic rule and populism are not antithetical to one another, but rather have come to complement each other as modes of rule. Much like New Labour in the UK and the Five Star Movement in Italy, Macron's LREM has come to exemplify a mode of political agency which combines these two aspects of political rule: rule by merit and competence, and a claim to be representing the people as a whole rather than specific interests linked to socioeconomic status.

The technocratic credentials of the Macron régime are best illustrated not only in the person of the President but, rather, also in the members of the National Assembly that came to dominate the legislative branch. Ninety per cent of the representatives elected to the National Assembly in 2017 for LREM were drawn from the professional and managerial classes, which themselves represent only 13 per cent of the population (Bickerton and Invernizzi Accetti 2021, 65). These new representatives, most of whom had no political background or legislative experience, were selected precisely because they came from civil society – although from a particular section of it. The Macron boys, the group of political advisers who surrounded Macron as candidate and then as president from 2016, also reflect this drawing on technical expertise from the civil service and business world. These highly educated advisers, graduates of Sciences Po, ENA and École des hautes études commerciales de Paris (HEC), all in their thirties – with one exception – represented the youthful dynamism, desire for change and modus operandi of the new régime. Together, this new elite was to bypass traditional modes of organization and consultation, sidestepping the *corps intermédiaires*, the trades unions, civil society organizations, and political parties that had mediated interests until then. The régime became the leading advocate for unmediated relations between the rulers and the ruled, between Macron, his closest advisers and political allies and the people as a whole.

It would be too simplistic to merely view the organization of political rule under Macron as a top-down initiative. Although certainly the mode of rule is highly personal and centred around the figure of the President himself, there were numerous attempts at establishing grassroots movements around the vision of the President. During the campaign, Macron launched *La Grande Marche*, a fact-finding exercise to find out which priorities the French people desired. In response to the *gilets jaunes* movement, he called for *Le Grand Débat National*, during which he toured France and spoke to mayors about their concerns. In 2019, he called for a *Convention Citoyenne pour le Climat*, a randomly selected group of citizens tasked with finding solutions to the climate emergency. These three initiatives point to the desire to go directly to the people, but also point to the highly mediated nature of the technopopulist rule. Instead of mediation through political parties or other civil society organizations, the Macron régime sought to go directly to the people – although it controlled the selection criteria, the summary of findings, and the interpretation of the data gathered. Creating the semblance of direct democracy, these initiatives in fact confirmed the highly concentrated nature of rule, with all of the information mediated through Macron's inner circle. This was justified in terms of their high levels of competence and unique ability to engage with the people in a direct manner as experts capable of divining the millions of contributions into a coherent programme.

The meritocratic belief at the root of this technopopulism is itself ideological. We do not live in a post-ideological world, where politics has vanished to leave room to competent managers who know best how to interpret the wishes of the people. At the root of the issue is the belief that the entire body of the population can be represented by a single, problem-solving, and technical body of experts that find technical solutions to issues. The consensus-centred approach is, of course, not unique to Macron and his régime. In many ways, it is symptomatic of a larger phenomenon, which Bickerton and Invernizzi Accetti detail in their book. While I do not disagree with their framing of technopopulism *per se* when they describe it as non-ideological in its operational status to reflect its broad appeal through various movement from New Labour to the Five Star Movement, I have unearthed the particular ideological roots it takes in Macron's France, as a mode of rule based on a particular conception of human teleology rooted in deep theological concepts. The section of the population that Macron's régime best represents – the professional and managerial classes – themselves constitute a small minority of the French electorate and public. Yet they claim to represent France as a whole, unmediated by the burdens of political representation and traditional conflict. They possess the grace to make sense of a world they claim to be post-ideological, chosen for their individual brilliance, skill, and success. They have climbed to the top of a highly meritocratic education system, and then proven themselves as entrepreneurs of their own selves to be worthy of the trust put in them by the people. They run France as a start-up nation, in a similar manner than a young tech-savvy person sees a niche in the market and comes up with a new product that revolutionizes an industry. Their aim is nothing less than revolution. Their methods are themselves a shattering of the old-world order, starting with the demise of political parties and other organizations of group interest and representation. Their promise is one of transcendence of past grievances through the creation of a new France. With such high expectations and goals, failure is not an option; for the fall will be as expedient as the rise, the crash as brutal as the reforms, the disillusionment as potent as the hope.

4

Hope

In his New Year's message for 2022, Macron wished for a better world for the coming year: '2022 can be the year of the end of the pandemic, I want to believe it with you; the year where we can see the light at the end of the tunnel' (Élysée 2021), before declaring in March, barely two months later: 'The war in Europe is no longer that of history books, it is here, under our noses' (Élysée 2022). The dichotomy of political affects into hope and fear plays directly to the liberal dream put together by Macron. His is the party of hope, the party of an open society, pro-European, globalist, based on free markets and rewarding merit. It is portrayed as the answer to the fear-driven, nationalist, Eurosceptic ideology of the far right that is driven by cronyism, nepotism and corruption. This hope/fear dichotomy obfuscates the interplay between those two emotions, that there is no hope without fear or fear without hope, and that basing a political programme on hope has the potential for dramatic disillusionment in the case where those hopes are shattered by the unfolding of events. By introducing the concept of hope as an affect, as an emotion which drives action, and its relation to fear, the first part of this chapter will show that understanding Spinoza and Nietzsche on the concept will go a long way to highlight some of its pitfalls. We will then see how hope was deployed, by Macron, to achieve his political aims.

Hope as affect

In his *Ethics*, Spinoza defines hope as 'an inconstant pleasure, arising from the idea of something past or future, whereof we to a certain extent doubt the issue' (2003). Hope is a pleasure, something we take comfort and derive a psychological good from. Hope is also about things that are outside of our control: it is an affect of the lack of power to influence the outcome of events. It is, ultimately, an emotion of impotence. But it is also a good for Spinoza, in that we derive pleasure from the reassurance that hope offers us about precisely those events over which we have no control over. We can only hope that the weather will not ruin our weekend picnic plans, or that our favourite team will win this year's championship, or that our carefully crafted plans for the future do not encounter insurmountable obstacles. Without hope, we would simply fear the outcome of those events which are outside our control. Whether we are waiting for news of something that has already happened, or lie in anticipation of some future event, neither of which we can affect, we can only hope or fear – and hope seems better than fear. But hope has a dark side. It is one of the passions, and forms part of Spinoza's affective theory more generally – together with fear, love and hatred. Hope is a type of pleasure caused by uncertainty, and as such can be fickle. It easily leads to disappointment once the idea we had of the past or future event turns out to have been untrue. A rainy Saturday, the repeated defeat of our sports team, or insurmountable hurdles ruining our plans can all crush hope out of existence and result in despair. This is already a first danger with the notion of hope – its uncertainty leads to a pleasure which can easily be turned into pain. The Ancient Greek myth of Pandora's box helps to illustrate this initial danger well. The myth takes the form of a struggle between Zeus, king of the Gods, and the Titan Prometheus. Prometheus, having given fire to humanity, angers Zeus, who decides to punish humanity by sending Pandora, the first woman, whose name signifies 'all gifts', and a jar to Epimetheus, Prometheus' brother. When the jar – what we call Pandora's box – is opened by Epimetheus, all of the evils of the world are released from it, with the notable exception of hope, which remains within the jar. Hesiod's narrative can be read in a number of ways, particularly with the meaning of hope it puts into question. Vincent Geoghegan (2008) proposes three readings of this role of hope in the myth: hope as the greatest calamity; hope as punishment; and hope as mercy. Let us explore those in turn.

Hope, in Nietzsche's interpretation of Pandora's box, is the greatest calamity for humanity. Although Hesiod mentions that Pandora was meant as a calamity for humanity, it is not clear that this applies to hope – which is the only evil that remains firmly inside the jar. Nietzsche's reading affirms that hope has been catastrophic for humanity. Humanity, particularly since the rise of Christianity, has considered hope a virtue, unaware that hope was in fact designed by the gods to torment them. Because hope always comes back, even in the face of disappointment, it is in fact the worst of all evils, as it prolongs humanity's torments, which are repeated ceaselessly by a willing, hopeful participant always waiting for improvement. Another, perhaps darker, interpretation of hope is that promulgated by Arthur Lovejoy and George Boas, who conceive of hope as inaccessible by design, providing evidence of 'the envious and monopolistic temper of the Gods' (Geoghegan 2008, 28). No future redemption is possible, according to their reading, with humanity condemned to yearning without the possibility of fulfilment. Humanity is condemned to hope and never see the objects of its desires come to fruition, damning it to eternal suffering, as even a fulfilled hope only creates novel and more unrealizable hopes for the future. The third reading, more favourable to Zeus, reads the existence of hope in the jar as mercy. Zeus merely wished to punish humanity without annihilating them, and the trapping of hope in the jar is a sign of protection rather than a continuation of the punishment. This reading is closer to that offered by Christianity, notably by Paul, for whom hope is a cardinal theological virtue, together with love and charity. What these three readings exemplify is that hope is an ambiguous concept. Although a theological interpretation of it as an act of mercy is possible, outside of Christian theology it is less believable as an interpretation. The first two of these interpretations are largely negative, conceiving of hope as a source of disappointment or calamity, whereas the third one is more positive, conceiving of hope as virtue to be cherished and cultivated.

Spinoza falls clearly within the side that considers hope as having potential negative connotations. Hope is a human – all-too-human – emotion, to be placed in the context of other affects. Just as we feel love and hate, desire or aversion towards others or towards objects, hope and fear work together in our field of emotions. Hope is an emotion felt in the face of uncertainty, as we have seen earlier. If we increase our certainty about the outcome of these otherwise unknown events, we start to feel confidence, the positive side of hope for Spinoza. Hope that turns out to have been true creates this state of being, this confidence that is clearly a positive affect as the uncertainty is replaced with certainty. The joy experienced by rain giving way to sunshine on a Saturday morning, the exhilaration of our team winning a crucial match, or the unfolding of events according to our plans can have a strong affective effect on us and our well-being. But just as love can lead to hatred when it is disappointed, hope turns to despair when it is taken over by fear. Fear is the mirror opposite to hope in Spinoza's thought: where hope is considered to be a set of pleasures created by uncertainty, fear is pain created by uncertainty. Once uncertainty is taken away from fear, once what we feared has turned out to be true, the feeling mutates into despair, the mirror opposite to confidence. This means that despair arises from hope's opposite, and whereas fulfilled hope could lead to a positive affect (confidence), fulfilled fear is thought to lead to a negative affect. Yet this is not the entire picture of despair in Spinoza. There is also another type of despair – that which arises directly from hope. If the uncertainty that made us hope in the first place disappoints us, we may still fall into despair following a heightened sense of hope. A second consecutive rainy weekend, yet another poor season for our favourite team, or the repeated failure of our plans to unfold in the face of adverse events can lead to a profound sense of negative affect. There is thus a double danger of despair: one coming from the fulfilment of fear, and one coming from the disappointment of hope. Out of these two, the second, the disappointment of hope turning into despair, is the most dangerous. All of these emotions – hope and fear, despair and disappointment – come,

Spinoza notes, from defective knowledge or the absence of power. The worst state of being, despair and disappointment, is the direct consequence of this absence of power. Not able to control their future, human beings are prone to fall into these emotional traps – with only confidence providing a positive outcome from this interplay of emotions.

Going beyond Spinoza, one can attempt to isolate a third type of emotion, defined not in terms of hope and fear, but rather as the absence of hope. In French as in other Latin languages, the terms 'hope' and 'despair' are linked semantically. *Espoir* and *désespoir*, hope and despair, are linked together as semantic opposites. But *désespoir* can also represent the absence of hope, rather than the disappointment of hope. It is in this sense that *désespoir*, or 'unhope', to coin an ugly term for it, can play a role in our affects. André Comte-Sponville (2011), in his *Traité du désespoir et de la béatitude* argues that this is in fact Spinoza's point. By pointing out that hope can be so dangerous, Spinoza puts together an affective theory where the virtues are conceived without recourse to hope. Hope may be a human – all-too-human – emotion, but humans can limit its nefarious influence on their everyday lives. By recognizing the dangers of hope, they can attempt to limit its power over their lives. A very stoic ideal in Comte-Sponville, unhope is the ability to limit our thinking about the future to what is in our power to do. Unhope is linked to beatitude, to a happiness coming from being blessed – typically by God. Comte-Sponville (2008), who described himself as a Christian atheist (culturally Christian, but without a belief in God), does not shy away from the theological consequences of his argument. Unhope and beatitude, for him, can only be achieved by a sense of *ataraxia*, an attempt to be content with what one already has and what one has been blessed with, rather than a cycle of hope and despair. Without pushing this analysis much further, it illustrates the possibility of thinking outside of the hope/despair or hope/fear dichotomies. Perhaps beatitude is possible, or perhaps a more political virtue can emerge from this refusal of the hope/despair dichotomy. I will come back to this later in this chapter, as solidarity seems to be an important synthesis to the political crisis unfolding between competing visions of the future.

Macron's hope

Macron's use of hope falls within the first interpretation of hope – that of Christianity – which seeks it as a virtue to be cherished. On 4 May 2017, just before the second round of the presidential election, which he won and which propelled him to the highest office in the land, Emmanuel Macron tweeted 'Hope is on the move. Thank you @BarackObama', embedding a video of support by the former American president, who said that Macron 'appeals to people's hopes, and not their fears. ... *En Marche. Vive la France*' (Macron 2017). One could not hope for a clearer endorsement, and Obama's own rhetoric of hope clearly resonated with, and was fully assumed by, Macron. Again, during his New Year's address to the French people on 31 December 2020, Macron expressed his 'wishes of hope' for 2021 (Carriat 2020).

> 'Hope is here. Hope is here in this vaccine that human genius created in merely a year. ... Hope is here, and it grows every day, with the recovery that shudders already in France which will enable us to invent a stronger, more innovative and fair economy. ... Hope lives in the freedom we will recover. ... Hope lives in our young people, of whom we have asked so much.' (France 24 2020)

The message of hope, expressed at a time of evening curfews and closed businesses, is representative of Macron's wider message of hope. In the face of adversity, difficulties and hardship, hope is here to give us a light at the end of the tunnel. The message could provide a much-needed, hopeful and confident perspective for the end of the drastic measures in place to fight the disease, but it could equally disappoint – with a new confinement declared in the spring of 2021 and a controversial 'health pass' introduced in the summer coming to disappoint these hopes. Instead of vaccines, economic recovery, freedom, and measures aimed at young people, the measures of hope promised by Macron in his New Year's wishes of 2021 turned out to be a world of bureaucratic control on the unvaccinated, rising inequalities, restrictions on movement and a disenfranchised youth. These made the fall into despair inevitable after disappointed hopes for the second year of fighting the virus.

Macron's message of hope is not limited to the response to the pandemic. It was always part of his programme, and part of the vision of the future promoted as candidate, as president, and as a wider political ideology. Among those who defend this ideology, such as Pedder, the message of hope is part of the appeal of Macron's politics. 'Macron's attempt to fashion a progressive, European alterative, infused with a message of hope, was both a means of remaking party politics and a response to the populist threat' (Pedder 2018, 76). As Spinoza had noted, hope requires fear to function, and Macron's message of hope is first and foremost an alternative to the fear of the FN in 2016–17 (now the RN). Against the perceived rise of populism à la Le Pen, Macron proposes a hope that reinforces the opposite values to those of his opponent. Against national preference, he reinforces the need for a better and stronger Europe. Against a predominantly older electorate for the far right, he proposes a message of hope for France's youth. Against the fear of the far right gaining power, he posits himself as the only alternative to the descent into chaos. Fear is thus mobilized within the message of hope – fear of an even worse political outcome, with Macron portrayed as the candidate of last hope *par excellence*. This message of hope, 'to become a Barack Obama *à la française*' (Pedder 2018, 121), contrasts badly with a French philosophical tradition sceptical of appeals to theological virtue. Victor Hugo, who defended melancholy as the happiness of being sad, and Jean-Paul Sartre and Simone de Beauvoir, who adopted *ennui* as a way of life, are much more representative of the French philosophical tradition than Macron's appeal to hope suggests, as Pedder (2018, 127) herself notes. Comte-Sponville, who defends unhope as desperation, can be added to that long list of French intellectuals who are hostile to the message of hope. Hope is too crass, too naïve for the rationalist philosophers, always critical of promises for a better future based on an appeal to the emotions. Macron's message is clearly against the current of this French philosophical tradition, perhaps to his advantage in electoral politics. Hope can be a powerful motivator, as Spinoza himself agrees, especially once it is turned into confidence. Both Barack Obama and Emmanuel Macron, who campaigned on this message of hope, show that it has potential as an electoral strategy. The issue comes when hopes turn to disappointment and despair, when the hopes that were raised to astronomical levels by the revolutionary vision of a new candidate coming from the margins of the political establishment turn out to promote the interests of those who are at the very top of that establishment. Barack Obama's message of hope paved the way for the fear-driven politics of Donald Trump in the US, and Emmanuel Macron's hopes have seen a dramatic rise in the popularity of far-right, fear-driven candidates standing in the 2022 election, such as Éric Zemmour and Marine Le Pen.

In Macron's electoral programme/autobiography, the term 'hope' appears almost nowhere, but hope is infused in every corner of the text. It is the central message of the chapter 'Caring for France' (*Vouloir la France*) that hope for a better future is the only rampart against extremism. The level of fear is raised by the candidate, with risks described everywhere for an ailing France. Civil war looms on the horizon; foreign powers plan attacks from the outside while domestic terrorists attack us from within; a 'totalitarian death project' – Islamic terrorism – is at play, using resentment and a hatred of the Republic against those who care for France (Macron 2016, 170). Our *banlieues* have become ghettos, where mass unemployment is the norm, leaving us 'not knowing how to give hope to millions of young people' (Macron 2016, 171). Hope must therefore, first and foremost, come from education and work opportunities. With regards to education and professional training, Macron is adamant that this is the only way for the French economy to compete on a global market. Credentialism may be the last accepted prejudice of today, as we have seen in Chapter 2, and those without an education only have themselves to blame for their misery. But that does not absolve Macron from promoting a more competitive education economy. If education is lagging behind in France, it can be reformed through public investment in primary schools, and a reform of higher education to better meet the demands of the knowledge economy. Hope is placed first and foremost in France's young population – those malleable enough to accept the realities of global markets and competition, those not yet entrenched in their corporatist or political interests. But the apotheosis of hope comes with the entrepreneur – the bearer of expectations for the future, the priest of the religion of hope, the apostle of future expectations.

Why the French don't have a word for entrepreneur

The French, famously, don't have a word for entrepreneur, George W. Bush is credited as saying. This tongue-in-cheek statement reflects a particular attitude towards and perception of the French, although the economic reality is far from the stereotype. The French model of capitalism has been notoriously slow to keep pace with the world of start-ups, venture capital and unicorns (the famous start-ups valued at more than $1 billion). One of the biggest complaints of Macron the candidate was that France does not allow for economic risk, activity, and hope from its entrepreneurial base. The cost of terminating work contracts is too high, the cost of labour is too high, regulations are too cumbersome, trades unions too powerful, unemployment benefits too high and social protection antiquated, Macron claimed in his chapter titled 'Making a Living' in one of the most Newspeak chapters of the book (Macron 2016, 119–33). Although figures for start-ups were by no means catastrophic for France in 2017, with unicorns such as Blablacar and OVHcloud showing signs of growth in their sectors prior to Macron's election, and investment levels higher than those found in neighbouring Germany (Agnew 2017), the message of hope was best served by claiming the apocalyptic state of French entrepreneurial spirit, and its need for deep and radical rejuvenation – primarily through a deep reform of the labour market in favour of employers. Hope always comes hand in hand with fear – the fear of French entrepreneurial *déclassement*, of the mass exodus of French entrepreneurs seeking their fortune elsewhere, and of a world where the French are better known for their strikes and street protests than for their luxury-brand industry and Michelin-starred restaurants.

For all of their traditional scepticism in the face of hope, their hostility to ostentatious signs of wealth, and attachment to traditions ill suited to the fast-paced economics of the entrepreneurial ethos, the French are also known for electing the candidate of hope in 2017, for their world of luxury and for the marketing of their *savoir vivre*. The richest person in the world was, for a brief period at the high of lockdowns during the global pandemic, Bernard Arnault, a Frenchman who is the founder of the LVMH group and close to Emmanuel Macron (Forbes 2021). In 2017, Arnault published a piece in *Les Échos* (a newspaper he owns) detailing why he voted for Macron in the first round of the presidential election, urging his readers to follow suit for the second round. Against the 'dead branch' of Marine Le Pen's Front National, Arnault (2017) foresaw the 'brand of hope and reason' of Emmanuel Macron. The 'foundational conviction' that both Arnault and Macron share, according to the former, is the 'conviction that private enterprise constitutes the only efficient lever for the durable, healthy and massive creation of employment in France.' The heroic entrepreneurs who are at the forefront of this creation have to face the hurdles of 'unreasonable fiscal policy' and 'procedural bureaucracy', the two enemies of hope, for a prosperous economic future. One can hardly blame Arnault for voting for Macron: he benefited from tax breaks under the new president. Yet his attack on the state is hypocritical at best, as LVMH had in the 1980s largely benefited from public subsidies and help from the French state without which Arnault could not have prospered (Lamm 2007). In line with the definition of neoliberalism we discussed in Chapter 1, the vision of society promoted by Arnault and Macron is one where entrepreneurs are given public help, but also benefit from a largely regressive fiscal environment where they contribute less to the public purse than well-paid professionals. The hope that justifies this recourse to increasingly inegalitarian measures is the hope that these entrepreneurs are the sole creators of jobs in the modern economy. This hope is defended tooth and nail, as a conviction that is portrayed as a fact, when in reality it remains full of uncertainty.

There are known knowns, known unknowns, and unknown unknowns, to paraphrase the political philosophical wisdom of former US Secretary of Defence Donald Rumsfeld. Rumsfeld's point, in his defence of the US military strategy towards Iraq in the build-up to the invasion, was that we might not even know what we don't know – there can be so much uncertainty that every decision about the future is bound to be imperfect. Rumsfeld's omission, however, is clear: he never talks about unknown knowns, the fourth epistemological category in his model. What about things which we think we know, but in fact do not know? Macron's recourse to hope as a form of conviction falls within this category of unknown knowns, deeply held convictions and beliefs that are in fact uncertain speculations about the future. In ordinary parlance, we tend to think of these unknown knows as the domain of faith: the belief that belief itself is valuable, that without a belief in the power of belief we are doomed to despair. If we believe hard enough in the truth of the economic trickle-down redistribution of wealth, it will become true. If those at the top of economic structure believe in the theory, they will act upon it and make it true in practice. When Arnault claims that he shares this conviction with Macron, he is being genuine – he believes that those most economically successful such as himself are best placed to create the economy of the future. And both

Arnault and Macron surely believe in a form of progressive values coming from this trickle-down conception of economics. With those at the top creating more jobs, better-skilled workforces and more competitive practices, everyone benefits from this economic reality. In fact, as Piketty (2013) points out at length, low wealth taxes and fiscal advantages for the top 1 per cent of earners – successful entrepreneurs, among others – have led to the rise of inequality since the 1980s, whether in Reagan's United States, Blair's United Kingdom, or Mitterrand's France. The conviction that wealth is best created and distributed by successful economic actors is precisely a type of faith, an unknown known – which has little historical evidence to justify it.

The future, of course, does not merely repeat the past. There is always the hope to create a better system of trickle-down economics, one that is more efficient, more redistributive and more progressive. This is part of Macron's faith in a better future, where a light-touch public sector encourages virtuous economic behaviour and discourages vices. The abolition of the ISF was meant to provide such nudges to the top 1 per cent of earners. After a few very public defectors made their discontent about French wealth taxes known in 2013, such as the actor Gérard Depardieu, who became a Russian citizen, and Bernard Arnault, who applied (but then withdrew his application) for Belgian citizenship, the suppression of the ISF came as a desire to make the tax more efficient by preventing this exodus of the wealthy. This was an act of faith, as the facts contradict this vision of French society being rejected by the country's top earners. The fiscal collections from the ISF itself had quadrupled in size since its introduction under Mitterrand, outpacing economic growth. In a world where inequalities are rising, the tax (which always remained fairly modest in terms of its economic impact) was failing to redress its redistributive purpose, as fortunes were rising much more quickly than what the tax took away from top earners. Furthermore, it was not the most progressive tax at the very top – with the top 1 per cent paying relatively more than the top 0.1 per cent, meaning the rich were paying more than the very rich. Reports that the abolition of the ISF would save Bernard Arnault €500 million were wildly exaggerated, as they assumed he was paying the tax on his entire fortune, which was not the case. In 2015, Arnault paid only €2.24 million on the ISF – more than two hundred times less than one would expect from the size of his estate (Les Décodeurs 2018). This tax optimization is perfectly legal and does not constitute tax evasion; it is merely the application of the law, which Macron considered too punitive for the economically successful. According to Bruno Le Maire, the French economy minister, the top 100 ISF taxpayers contributed €126 million to the public purse: in other words, Arnault was not an isolated case but representative of what this tax cost billionaires in France: about €1 million each. For others who were paying the tax, the average saving from the tax's abolition was €9,700 – for a tax that begins on assets exceeding €1.3 million.

In other words, the tax — which was itself regressive between those with assets worth around a million euros who paid just under 1 per cent a year and those worth billions who paid less than 0.1 per cent a year — was symbolic rather than economically crippling for anyone paying it. Its suppression was an act of faith rather than based on evidence — it aimed to nudge the top 1 per cent of earners to do more for society, by giving them a tax break they could reinvest in the economy. Meanwhile, GDP per capita in France has not risen for over a decade and was lower in 2020 than in 2007, with disproportionate growth favouring those at the very top, meaning a lowering of living standards for most of the population. The rising tide has failed to materialize, disappointing the hope of those who have been on the receiving end of these rising inequalities.

Hope and community

By framing ideological convictions as facts, Macron merely continued what others did before him: turning a political choice towards increased inequalities and a business-friendly government into a technical solution to an apolitical problem. What is portrayed as a known is actually an unknown, what is shown as the only reasonable choice is an ideological position, what is given as a conviction is an act of faith, what is claimed as certain is merely hope. The biggest danger with hope in politics is the disappointment that comes from its lack of success. Since hope is created under conditions of uncertainty, any hope that fails to fulfil its promises can lead to a catastrophic fall into despair. When hope is elevated into a political virtue, it turns this potential danger of despair into a near certainty. In politics, someone is always going to be disappointed by the promises of hope. This is not necessarily because politics is a zero-sum game, but because we cannot reasonably expect everyone to be aligned in their beliefs and conceptions of the good life. Politics will always create dissention and discord, even in the best of circumstances. Under the difficult circumstances faced during Macron's presidency — with a global pandemic hitting a country that had yet to recover from a large economic recession — hope turned out to be a *faux ami*, not a virtue but the setting up of despair. Hope can, and sometimes does, work in politics. In the face of national disasters, hope may be the only feeling keeping a people together. Hope could have been a powerful motivator during COVID-19, if all had felt they were held together by a common purpose and sacrifices. But if hope falls short of its promises, it can also undo much of the social bond, create fear and exacerbate existing divisions.

Hope as a virtue has long been defended not only in Christian theology, but also in political practice. Barack Obama best illustrates the message of hope as a political virtue, the defence of the affective power of hope in the American psyche. Even before he ran for president, Obama publicly defended his message of hope. At the 2004 Democratic National Convention, he gave a speech defending presidential candidate John Kerry's record in giving America hope. By hope, Obama insisted, he did not mean inaction or wishful thinking, but something of substance.

> 'It's the hope of slaves sitting around a fire singing freedom songs. The hope of immigrants setting out for distant shores. The hope of a young naval lieutenant bravely patrolling the Mekong Delta. The hope of a mill worker's son who dares to defy the odds. The hope of a skinny kid with a funny name who believes that America has a place for him, too ... The audacity of hope!' (cited in Frank and McPhail 2005)

The message of hope was further amplified in Obama's (2008) book, whose title he had already hinted at a couple of years earlier. The message of hope is clearly anchored in the self-perception of American greatness by its elected officials. What makes the United States such a special place, worthy of exceptionalism, is the hope it gives to all those who are willing to accept the American dream. The slave, the soldier, the working person, the marginalized, can all make it equally, through hard work and talent. It is the ideal of merit described in Chapter 2, the one best illustrated by Benjamin Franklin's writings according to Max Weber. 'That was the best of the American spirit, I thought – having the audacity to believe despite all the evidence to the contrary that we could restore a sense of community to a nation torn by conflict' (Obama 2008, 356).

Hope is not only shared among progressive liberals but is infused in the work of socialist thinkers too. Ernst Bloch (1995) defended ardently the principle of hope from the left. Hope is stronger than fear, hope is emancipatory, hope is a remedy for anxiety about life, hope is teachable. We all daydream about the future, according to Bloch, but we can be taught to daydream better, so that these dreams grow fuller, clearer, less random, more clearly understood. Hope, for Bloch, is about planning for the future without ever being associated with planning committees or a one-party state. It is mediated through reason but also through the material conditions of those who daydream and labour for a living. It is summarized by the ontological notion of the Not-Yet. Hope is about what could be but has not yet been brought forth. The wished-for, better life lies in anticipation for Bloch, giving it a particularly difficult epistemological status. How are we to know what is Not-Yet? Through utopia, conceived widely to reflect not only literary works but utopian thinking in medical, social, technological, architectural and geographic utopias. What Bloch calls hope is more akin to social planning, to the elaboration of blueprints for a future architecture, to the elaboration of workplace relations free of exploitation. There is no sign of this aesthetic of hope in Macron, of utopian thinking planning for a better future. Macron's vision of the future is more akin to a dystopian landscape, where the French work longer, for less pay, to finance the rise of their owner-entrepreneurs.

In Bloch, hope always maintains a certain religious dimension. Karol Wojtyła, Pope John Paul II (1994), wrote about his message of hope in *Crossing the Threshold of Hope*. For His Holiness, hope is to be placed in the young, remembering the young's role in the Warsaw Uprising of 1944 where young heroes laid down their lives against the occupiers; before lamenting the materialist culture of today's youth (Paglia 1994). Emmanuel Macron, who came from a non-religious family but insisted on being baptized into the Catholic faith, is now an agnostic. He may not know about the nature of God, but he has held on to the message of hope found in the adopted faith of his youth. In a secular country such as France, where atheists are everywhere and Catholics feel like they are in a minority in their own country (Gugelot 2017), the agnostic Macron is perfectly placed to straddle the divide between the two groups. The atheist left and the Catholic right have found their central ground in the agnostic Catholicism of Macron, with a message of secularized hope that appeals to both groups from the centre ground.

Changing *laïcité*

That messages of hope work in the United States is not surprising. Americans are much more open to religiously inspired messages than then French, who maintain a strong attachment to their unique model of secularism – *laïcité*. The edict of Nantes of 1598 signed by Henri IV, and its subsequent revocation by his grandson Louis XIV in 1685, provided initial roots for secularism in France, as well as a reaction to the separation of Church and State. The French Revolution continued this legacy of secularism, through nationalizations of Church property, again followed by a reaction to this separation under Napoleon, who put control of French churches firmly under the state's authority. The current model of *laïcité* is more recent, dating back to the law of 1905 and its formal separation of the Napoleonic marriage of the French state and its churches. The law itself has acquired the status of quasi-myth in the French psyche, referred to colloquially as *la loi de 1905* – *the* law of 1905 – as if no other laws were passed that year. Although the law itself did formally separate the French state and churches, was a marked difference from the previous system of the *concordat* and was furiously disputed by the Pope Pius X, it was also a compromise between radical republicans and liberally minded Catholics in France. It ended the French state's financing of churches, notably by no longer employing priests, bishops, ministers and rabbis directly – and thus renouncing its ability to nominate bishops – but it also conferred on churches notable fiscal and financial advantages, exempting them from taxes on donations, for example.

While the law confirmed the nationalizations of church property during the Revolution, it also created cultural associations responsible for the maintenance of these properties, effectively subsidizing the maintenance of existing churches (the vast majority of them belonging to the Catholic Church). In short, the law was not a *strict* separation of Church and State, but rather a political compromise, in the context of the Third Republic, which limited the role of the Catholic Church in French public life – but strengthened its ability to operate as an independent institution with financial support and fiscal exemptions. A portion of the French Catholic clergy, most notably Louis Duchesne, as well as Protestant churches and Jews, welcomed the law as providing enough guarantees for freedom of worship – although relations with the Holy See in Rome were not restored formally until after the First World War.

In contemporary French politics, the compromise of 1905 is more often than not treated as a strict and inflexible separation of religion and politics – particularly in the French state and society's stance on Islam. The most divisive issue over the past decades has been the wearing of veils, niqabs and burqas by Muslim women, ignited by the refusal of three girls to remove their veil in class in 1989. The girls were expelled from their school in the commune of Creil, in the *département* just north of Paris, starting a national debate on whether *laïcité* is compatible with the wearing of face coverings in public. The political climate around Islam was particularly tense at the time. Salman Rushdie had just published his *Satanic Verses*, leading to calls for a fatwa against him by Ayatollah Khomenei. Political debates raged around the issue, until the *Conseil d'État* deliberated on it in November of that year, determining that the expression of religious identity could not be forbidden in schools. The girls went back to school, and the debate subsided but never quite disappeared (Blavignat 2018). The French position was then reversed, in 2004, in an equally tense context – after 9/11 and Western interventions in Afghanistan and Iraq. The law, which forbade the wearing of 'ostentatious' religious symbols in public schools (while still permitting 'discreet' signs of religious affiliation) was widely perceived as targeting Muslim girls and young women, as it clearly applied predominantly to the wearing of the hijab. It notably did not challenge the wearing of small crosses, indulging the dominant religion while imposing strict controls on others. Defended by liberals as reasonable in the context of minors in publicly financed schools (Weil 2009), the measure soon escalated beyond the strict context of public education. In 2010, a law extended the banning of face coverings in public, notably meant to prevent women from wearing the niqab or burqa in public – despite very few women wearing them in France at the time. In 2016, a number of mayors and prefects introduced bans on the wearing of *burkinis*, swimwear worn by some Muslim women on public beaches. Though the *Conseil d'État* struck down the interdiction as it was deemed to pose no significant threat to public order, it was an object of debate during the presidential election of 2017. Emmanuel Macron, debating with Le Pen, notably defended the right of mayors to ban burkinis, claiming some of the decisions were justified (Quinault-Maupoil 2017). 'The burkini is a problem', then presidential candidate Macron claimed. Images of the previous summer, where police officer were forcing women to undress on beaches to apply the decisions of local officials, were justified by Macron. This security state was not incidental, but always defended as a necessary feature of his liberal politics.

France's *laïcité* has changed, notably since 2004 and the first law which regulated how individuals can dress. But while secularism has been strengthened in its approach to Islam, there has been a growth in the importance of religion in French politics. This is perhaps the most glaring feature of the new French secularism – that it has favoured a return to the religious in public life, despite the claim to have separated the religious from the political. The most notable example is the opposition to homosexual marriage, which grew into the *La Manif pour tous* in 2012. When newly elected François Hollande began the legislative process to introduce his 'marriage for all', its opponents gathered around the 'demonstration for all'. The movement was meant to be inclusive, allegedly comprised of 37 groups including homosexuals against marriage, education groups and legal practitioners, as well as feminist organizations and a Muslim organization. But an investigation by the newspaper *Le Monde* revealed that most of these groups were only Facebook pages or individuals having created a website – the real organizing power of the Manif Pour Tous being the Catholic Church and its members (Laurent 2013). Between November 2012 and October 2014, the collective organized a series of demonstrations, with up to a million demonstrators at the height of the movement according to the organizers. It was certainly one of the most important social movements since the events of 1968, on a similar scale to the *gilets jaunes* who operated during Macron's presidency. The Catholic Church still has political power in France – through its members and through its capacity to organize a social movement of almost unparalleled size and level of activity. It is not a surprise that the main right-wing candidate for the presidential election of 2017, François Fillon, was himself an outspoken Catholic (a rare sight in French politics), a defender of family values and largely favoured by the Catholic electorate (Tresca 2017). Only the political scandal of his fictive employment of family members, notably his wife Penelope who was his parliamentary assistant despite there being no evidence that she did any work. 'Penelopegate', as the Fillon affair became known, set the stage for the results of the first round of the presidential election in 2017. Eclipsed by Le Pen, Fillon was knocked out of the election despite having been favourite in the polls in 2016. François and Penelope Fillon were found guilty by a court in

2020 and condemned to five and three years in prison, respectively, as well as ordered to pay fines and reimburse the National Assembly almost €2 million. Without the scandal around these fictive jobs, one can only speculate as to how the election of 2017 would have turned out. With Le Pen positioning herself as the defender of a particular type of secularism – one that wants to enforce strict controls on religion, but also to allow local municipalities to install nativity scenes on their premises, she was able to gather the votes of the *catholaïques* – French Catholics attached to secularism particularly when it applies very strictly to Islam.

Macron himself has continued this trend of the new French *laïcité,* which cajoles the Catholic electorate while targeting Islam. His administration passed a law on separatism which clearly targets Muslims and poses particular issues for the finance and organization of Islam in France. Jonathan Laurence (2021) makes this point in his opinion piece to the Catholic newspaper *La Croix*. The consequences of the law, which attempts to sever ties between French Islam and its international counterparts, will lead to a weakening of spiritual resources for Muslims, according to Laurence. Who will train the new imams, finance their seminary, or pay their salaries if all foreign funding ceases? By treating Islam in the same way as it treated the Catholic Church in the late nineteenth century and early twentieth century, the French state is attempting a one-size-fits-all approach to religious denominations, one that is particularly ill suited to the needs of French Muslims. Unlike French Catholicism over a century ago, French Islam suffers a lack of capacity to organize itself. It lacks the means to train its own imams, to organize its interests, and to defend them through political channels. Motivated by the spectacular beheading by a Chechen Islamist of a high school teacher who had shown his students *Charlie Hebdo* cartoons depicting the Prophet Muhammad in a class on freedom of expression, the law on separatism has the unfortunate consequence of weakening the voices in French Islam that combat these extremist views. Macron, a firm defender of *laïcité* (a prerequisite for elected public office in France), thus continued the trend of the past two decades to mutate French secularism into one that is increasingly hostile towards Islam, whilst taking great pains to cosy up to the Catholic electorate that is becoming increasingly more self-assertive.

Charity

The hope that Macron promotes is itself a secularized version of Catholic hope. Its chief aim is not to restore the hope in God or in the Church but to introduce a new secularized hope. The entrepreneur is the best figure of this secular hope, whose mechanism is the act of willing. The will is such an important part of Macron's vision of the world that it appears in the title of two of the sixteen chapters that put forward his vision of the future in 2016. 'The France that We Want' and 'Caring for France' frame the importance of willing, for the entrepreneur and beyond. Against the perceived ills of French society, namely 'a thousand situations of unjustified rents', an 'unbearable [public] debt', social *déclassement*, 'massification' and 'egalitarianism', Macron proposes a model for an 'economy of innovation' (Macron 2016, 65–71). The France that he wills is one where 'corporatist protections have given way to individual securities'. In other words, the social protections of yesteryear need to go – unemployment insurance, generous pensions and safe employment should all be replaced with strict protections of property rights. This project, Macron (2016, 74) warns us, 'will take ten years' – and can only be achieved with a second mandate as President. The act of willing takes an important role here: only those who have a vision for the future, a hope in the power of the market to regulate social relations, and a willingness to crush the old régime of social and employment protections can move France forward. France itself, Macron (2016, 169) tells us, 'is a will'. Such a vision of France is best understood through the great men (and a token woman) who have willed France into what it is today. Macron's vision of history is also one of will: 'Clovis, Henri IV, Napoleon, Danton, Gambetta, de Gaulle, Joan of Arc, the soldiers of Year II [of the Revolution], Senegalese *tirailleurs*, Resistance fighters' (Macron 2016, 176) are the great persons who willed France in the past. The contemporary equivalent of these men of strong will is the entrepreneur, the CEO, who is much more than the mere *homo economicus* seeking to maximize profits. The entrepreneurs are the ones who carry the essential values of the France of the future. These values are, not surprisingly, theological. 'The mystery, transcendence, the intimate are, in everyday life, elements that cannot be summed up by money, social status or efficiency' (Macron 2016, 178). The mystery that is willing France is thus a much more all-encompassing role for the entrepreneur. The entrepreneur is not merely someone who contributes to the bottom line of the CAC40 (the French stockmarket index), who makes profits for shareholders and creates wealth. The entrepreneur is the cornerstone of this mystery of social hope. This mystery will take place not through the defence of social rights and protections, but rather through charity and the growth of the non-governmental sector.

In Macron's vision, all fraternity is resolved through volunteering in the charity sector. This focus on charity is itself deeply reactionary in its outlook. In *Anarchy, State and Utopia*, Robert Nozick (2001) had put forward such a libertarian vision of society, where the minimal state takes no role in social spending but provides the basis for a purely voluntary and charitable mode of solidarity. But it is in the thought of Edmund Burke that one finds the early and deeply conservative roots of charity as a mode of solidarity. Already defending the principle of charity against state intervention in his parliamentary career, Burke expressed his views in 1774 when the British parliament was debating a reform to the Elizabethan Poor Law. During the debate, Burke attacked the general principles of the law, according to which the poor, that is, those unable to sustain themselves, could seek to be maintained by the better-off in their parish. Burke's argument against the Poor Law was that it was 'converting "the voluntary, free duty of Charity" into "a tax for the poor"' instead of "compassion", people felt "abhorrence, and dread"' (Lock 2008a, 359). Burke preferred charity over taxation because, in his view, it was not the role of government to find a solution to poverty. Poverty was part of the natural order of things. In *Reflections on the Revolution in France,* perhaps the best tract of conservative political ideology, Burke even defends the Gallican Church, and in particular its monastic orders, on the basis that they are well suited to providing charity. This is surprising, given the Anglican Church's hostility to the 'lazy monks'. He notes that, not unlike the trickle-down of the capitalist owners, the monastic orders, however lazy, will devote their surplus 'to charitable, cultural or educational projects: on magnificent buildings, on excellent libraries and the patronage of art, on scholarship and scientific research' (Lock 2008b, 305). Burke was not entirely wrong: among the contributors to Diderot and D'Alembert's *Encyclopédie* figured the abbots Claude Yvon, Jean-Martin de Prades, Jean Pestré and Nicolas-Sylvestre Bergier. In *ancien régime* France, charity was often the only mode of subsistence for intellectual endeavours. Diderot himself spent most of the 20 years he worked on the *Encyclopédie* in poverty, depending on the generosity of his friend the Baron d'Holbach, and later on the largesse of the Empress of Russia, Catherine the Great. Burke's defence of charity culminated in his opposition to the British state's intervention in the famine of 1795. He 'vehemently opposed any attempt to supplement or subsidize wages from taxes, insisting that charity, not the State, must preserve the poor from starvation' (Lock 2008b, 318). Charity, not the state, is responsible for helping those in need. This is a foundational block of conservative ideology, and an important building block of the political right more generally. Charity acts as an ideological canary, providing early indications of the political orientation of a person or group. The closer they are to Burke, the more conservative they are in economic terms. Even for those who do not share Burke's otherwise conservative social outlook, the adoption of charity as a model for relieving suffering in society is indicative of a conception of society based on individual responsibility, the defence of existing property relations, and even a political theology based on Christian *caritas*.

Although most appeals to charity are secularized today, it is difficult not to notice the Christian origins of the practice as it stands. Building on the more ancient distinction between different types of love, the Christian notion of *caritas* builds on the Greek *agápē* as a form of unconditional love, different from *philia* (friendship) and *eros* (desire). In Christian theology, *agápē* becomes *caritas*, defined as the love of God for man, or of man for God. This divine love, or love of the divine, is charity. One shows one's love of God through charitable works, through helping others in need. It expresses a form of transcendence not found outside of this theological context. Even in its secularized version, charity maintains this political theological dimension. Charity replaces fraternity in Macron's thought, because it maintains a certain transcendental quality that he is clearly attached to. The advantage of charity as a social institution is that it maintains relations of power based on property relations. Those with significant wealth can decide where it is best used in charitable associations. They decide the priorities, the extent and the strength of their favourite causes, based on their inherent merit as successful social beings. Their largesse is determined by their will, as a level for social improvement but also as a stark reminder that their support can be withdrawn at any point – even for arbitrary reasons. It takes decision-making out of democratic hands when it comes to improving the social. Instead of a world where legislators can vote on priorities set by the state, charity firmly places decisions of who deserves to be saved into the private hands of successful individuals.

Conclusion

A world without hope need not be a world of despair. As we saw above, there are alternatives to hope as a political concept, such as Bloch's utopia or Comte-Sponville's unhope. Concrete examples of these alternatives include social models based on the ideal of solidarity. Progressive fiscal policy, public services for all, intergenerational justice can all form part of a vision of solidarity in the twenty-first century. Macron's philosophy of hope denies the possibility for any of these to take root. Global competitiveness, austerity, and a defence of settled property relations form the backbone of the economy for Macron's future. The social model *à la française*, based on the post-war settlement where economic actors accepted an in-between model based on a capitalist economic base with socialist social policies is in question today. In all fairness, this questioning started well before Macron came to power. Macron's ideology has the advantage of laying bare the relations of rising inequalities of this early twenty-first century. The future it promises is more dystopian than utopian, more apocalyptic than revolutionary. Solidarity is dead, to be replaced by hope, disillusionment, despair and fear. The affective cycle started by the return to hope can, however, be broken. There is still widespread appetite for a model of solidarity in France today. The institutions of public solidarity still enjoy widespread support. Unlike with hope, solidarity provides an ideal not dependent on success. Unlike the entrepreneur, the social worker, teacher, doctor, or public servant do not depend on the competitiveness of their activity. With successful economic activity comes increased mechanization and alienation from one's labour just as much as economic prosperity and the advantages of new technologies. Macron's ideology purports that solidarity must be trimmed down to make room for economic success. But his vision obscures the reality of economic success, which will require increased social care and solidarity. By proposing that hope replace solidarity, Macron is undermining the social fabric that becomes fragile precisely because of economic success. A vision for the future that combines solidarity and growth, economic success and support for those who do not succeed, this vision could have been Macron's centre-ground. But instead, Macron's ideology proposes the utter defeat of solidarity in the name of hope. What will happen next is not yet clear, but hope's dark side – despair, disillusionment and fear – is always lurking in the shadows.

Conclusion

The presidential elections of 2022 proved to be a testing ground for the central thesis of this book. The analysis above was largely finished – save for this conclusion – by the time the official campaign started on 28 March ahead of the two votes on 10 and 24 April. The ultimate victory of Emmanuel Macron repeated the 2017 result, albeit with important differences. The first difference was a shift of Macron's electorate to the right. Whereas Macron could still garner support from sections of the left in 2017, this support had virtually evaporated in 2022. It confirmed electorally what had already been true ideologically: Macron was now firmly the candidate of the right, crushing the old electoral right in 2022 as he had crushed the electoral left in 2017. The *bourgeois bloc*, now independent electorally, has largely rallied behind Macron and his values of security, merit and hope. The second difference was the antipathy of the left towards Macron. Even in the second round of the elections, more left-leaning voters shied away from giving Macron their support, recognizing that the next five years under Macron will be a continuation of the neoliberal reforms already enacted since 2017. Between the globalist neoliberal policies of Macron and the neoliberal nationalist policies of Le Pen, the choice for the left was unappealing, to say the least. This conclusion will detail those arguments by analysing the 2022 campaign and the results of the presidential elections, as well as providing some reflections on the future of French politics over the next five years. I will show that the best answer for the left during this period is to position itself as the alternative to Macron's new right, oppose its values and propose a positive alternative – notably by engaging the workers that abstain in large numbers in the electoral cycle.

The 2022 elections

France has a rather unique and original electoral cycle. The President of the Republic is elected directly by citizens, either in a single round of voting, in the case where a candidate gets over 50 per cent of the vote – something that has never happened in the history of the Fifth Republic, not even when de Gaulle ran for office – or in a face-off between the top two candidates in a second round of the election two weeks after the first round. All candidates need to secure 500 signatures from mayors to back their candidacy in order to run for the election, an obstacle for less prominent candidates who need to spend considerable resources talking to local officials and getting their patronage. There were 12 candidates in 2022, up from 11 in 2017, that met the conditions for candidacy. A thirteenth candidate, Christiane Taubira, came close to having collected the required 500 mayoral signatures, but pulled out of the race on 2 March 2022. She had won the 'popular primary', a failed attempt to have a single candidate for the left, with the main contenders to the presidential election not participating in the debates.

The presidential campaign itself continued some themes already present in 2017, and amplified others. The political left, in particular, came across as disunited. The revolutionary left, of Trotskyist persuasion, had fielded candidates for the past few elections, and 2022 was no exception. But even within this camp, disunity reigned. Two far-left candidates, Nathalie Arthaud and Philippe Poutou, represented two different branches of the revolutionaries. They each received less than 1 per cent of the vote. The PS candidate, Anne Hidalgo, the mayor of Paris, whose party was in power until Macron took office in 2017, was by far the largest failure on the left – she received below 2 per cent of the vote. The PS, which had already largely collapsed in 2017 with a mere 6 per cent of the vote in the presidential election that year, may be on the brink of bankruptcy after the 2022 elections. All parties that do not meet the 5 per cent threshold in the presidential elections face financial difficulties, as most state funding for the campaign is dependent on parties meeting this threshold. For a party that has given France presidents and prime ministers, the 2022 result marks the end of its role as the leading party of the left – if there was still any doubt after 2017. Hidalgo received fewer votes than the Communist (PCF) candidate, Fabien Roussel (2 per cent), and far fewer votes than she has Twitter followers (600,000 vs. 1.5 million). The communists, who had backed Mélenchon in 2012 and 2017 but ran a candidate in 2022, illustrate the further disunity of the left in France. Although the two parties, LFI and the PCF, could find common ground in the past, they split over a number of issues such as nuclear energy, 'wokeness' and hunting rights (Budgen 2022). In what seems to come out of a parody of political debates, Roussel clashed with the green politician Sandrine Rousseau over his defence of French wine, meat and cheese in what became briefly known as 'couscousgate', after Rousseau expressed her own preference for couscous as a more inclusive dish for vegetarians (Nicolas 2022). The divisions of the left are often based on the kind of differences linked to identity politics – with various sections of the left preferring one group over another. Yannick Jadot, the candidate for the green party (EELV), similarly split the vote on the left, as the greens had backed the PS candidate in 2017. The greens fared relatively well, outperforming the PS in 2022 with 4 per centof the vote.

But the main candidate of the left remained, as in 2017, Jean-Luc Mélenchon, who split from the PS in 2008 over disagreements regarding the EU (among other themes). Though he has toned down his anti-EU sentiment, Mélenchon remains a left-wing critic of the EU and proposes to renegotiate treaties or to disobey existing treaties if they go against his proposed policies. His policies, often described as far-left by the liberal press (White 2022), is typical of the left wing of social-democratic parties throughout the world. They resemble closely those of Bernie Sanders or Jeremy Corbyn, with calls for nationalization of key industries, a green new deal to push economic recovery, employment laws that favour employees over employers, and a higher minimum wage. Ultimately Mélenchon failed to reach the second round of the presidential elections, gaining only 22 per cent of the vote, just behind Marine Le Pen with 23 Per cent. Close, but no cigar. The six left candidates only gathered 32 per cent of the vote in the first round, far behind the candidates of the right and far right, with over 68 per cent. If Mélenchon had reached the second round of the presidential election, all polls pointed to a comfortable victory for Macron, with the hypothetical second round showing support for the outgoing president at between 57 per cent and 68.5 per cent.

The far right was also split during the election, although it fared much better electorally. Aurélien Mondon and Aaron Winter (2020) have analysed the rise of Jean-Marie Le Pen and then Marine Le Pen, his daughter, in the context of the normalization of far-right discourse in mainstream media and political discourse. What had already started in the 1980s under Mitterand's presidency has continued throughout the presidencies of his successors to the Élysée Palace. Mondon (2021) further explains how the favoured themes and political agenda of the far right have been adopted by the Macron presidency, thereby legitimating Le Pen's discourse and making it the natural opponent of his brand of liberalism. Macron's interior minister, Gérald Darmanin, notably attacked Le Pen for being 'too soft on Islam' in a debate on prime-time television; Macron himself embraced the old far-right conspiracy theory of 'Islamo-leftism', equating the left of the political spectrum with radical Islamist ideology; and an official account of the French government condemned the term 'Islamophobia' for being invented by Islamists to prevent criticism of Islam. This is without counting the law against separatism, passed under Macron's presidency and clearly targeting minority groups – particularly Islam – and widely threatening civil liberties (Khemilat 2021). As we saw in Chapter 2, the Macron régime has largely built the security apparatus of the state, one of the electoral strengths of the far right that has been campaigning against insecurity and in favour of the growth of the security functions of the state since its inception. Marine Le Pen capitalized on the breadth of media attention behind her candidacy, as well as the inclusion of themes close to her party's political alignment by mainstream parties, including Macron's LREM.

Marine Le Pen's biggest threat, in this election, came from her right – with the candidacy of Éric Zemmour threatening to outflank her and challenge the attempt by the RN to de-demonize itself. After Marine took over the presidency of the FN from her father Jean-Marie in 2011, she attempted to turn the page on the most distasteful aspect of the party – its antisemitism and defence of the Vichy régime, notably. The change in the party's name, following the defeat of 2017 in the second round of the presidential election, was the tip of the iceberg in this movement to change the image of the party into that of a respectable party of the French Republic. Members of the party were expelled, including Jean-Marie Le Pen himself, new recruits joined the party, notably in rural France and peri-urban areas, among the working classes and the middle classes (Challier 2017). The new militant base of the past decade has certainly changed some dynamics within the party, although the old guard has not been completely ousted from the party. Zemmour tried to capitalize on the disillusionment of the old guard, attracting some of them over to his side, such as Marion Maréchal, Le Pen's niece. Ultimately, Zemmour failed to convince, and lacked the local organization of the RN, coming fourth in the first round of the election with 7 per cent of the vote. Le Pen was also facing challenges from Nicolas Dupont-Aignan (2 per cent of the vote) and Jean Lassalle (3 per cent), who both campaigned on sovereignty platforms. The political right that openly challenges Macron's globalist preference remains a strong force in French politics, totalling 35 per cent of the vote in the first round.

Marine Le Pen ultimately failed to convince French voters that her project for France was better than Macron's. Although there were clear differences in terms of national preference versus support for the EU between Macron and Le Pen, both proposed a rather neoliberal approach to the state. Some have argued that Le Pen's programme is to the left economically, proposing a 'moderate redistributive programme of Keynesian orientation based on state interventionism, social protection and the defence of public services' (Fazi 2022). This analysis does not stand up to scrutiny, however. Le Pen's measures to restore purchasing power to the working classes are based on a neoliberal logic: that lowering taxes for businesses will trickle down to the lowest earners. One of her flagship measures, supposed to raise salaries by 10 per cent, is merely an incentive for employers to do so, promising tax breaks to achieve its means. It will not affect the minimum wage, as Lang (2022) has noted. Among her other 'social' reforms, the nationalization of motorways and higher spending in the health sector are two clear demagogic measures to capitalize on the two largest crises of the Macron régime – the *gilets jaunes* and the COVID-19 pandemic. They are not financed by any significant rise in taxation and, given her party's pro-austerity stance, do not raise hopes for a neo-Keynesian, tax-and-spend or coherent industrial policy for France. Whereas Macron proposed a globalist neoliberal economic model, Le Pen's alternative was to tip the balance slightly towards national preference in public procurement and weaken the state's capacity in terms of social provision and policies.

Emmanuel Macron barely campaigned in 2022. He announced his candidacy for re-election on the very day of the deadline, refused to debate other candidates ahead of the first round of the election, and only debated Marine Le Pen in a televised debate four days ahead of the final vote. The electoral strategy ultimately worked well for him – he did not have to face criticism from other candidates or defend his record, and only had to convince that he was the least bad of two options, beating the far right for a second time in a row. There are signs this was a deliberate strategy, with his close ally from the MoDem and former minister François Bayrou giving his mayoral backing to Le Pen ahead of her candidacy, and setting up a 'bank' of 365 mayoral votes to ensure that both Le Pen and Zemmour could stand as candidates in the election (*Le Figaro*, 2022). Justified on democratic terms, this electoral strategy boosted the far right, which otherwise struggles with getting enough support to field its candidates and has to expend large resources to guarantee its candidacies to the election.

> Back in 2017 you could still have people who were deluded in the idea that Macron was a kind of left/right mixture and there would be some good stuff for the left and some good stuff for the right … Those illusions have been completely destroyed over the last five years. (Bickerton 2022)

The ideology described in this book showed that Macron was always a candidate of the right. But the electoral maths showed that there was some support from the left in the 2017 elections, even in the first round of the election as the wealthier sections of the political left – *la gauche caviar* [or 'latte socialists'] – flocked to Macron for his first election. But in the 2022 elections, the shift to the electoral right had been almost complete, showing that voters had clearly understood, after five years in power, the ideology of the new right proposed by Macron. Out of those who had voted for Hollande, the PS candidate in 2012, 47 per cent voted for Macron in 2017, preferring him to their own party's candidate that year, Benoît Hamon. Voters who considered themselves 'on the left' (23 per cent) or 'slightly to the left' (47 per cent) also backed Macron in important numbers in 2017 (Ipsos 2017). This electorate did not repeat the trend in 2022. The transfer of votes from left parties to Macron in 2022 was low – only 22 per cent of those who had voted for the greens and 24 per cent of those who had voted for the PS in 2017 transferred their votes to Macron in 2022. On the other hand, the transfer of the vote from 2017 Fillon voters, whose candidate had come third, largely went to Macron with 32 per cent preferring the incumbent president over the candidate of their own party, Valérie Pécresse, who only received 29 per cent of the vote of her predecessor (Ipsos 2022). What Macron had achieved in 2017 with regards to the left – hollowing out the *bourgeois class* electorate of the PS – he replicated on the right in 2022, splitting the vote of the traditional party of power on the right, LR, and largely seducing its electors to join his ranks. The results of the second round of the presidential elections also confirmed this trend, with fewer left-leaning voters casting their vote for Macron in 2022 than in 2017. Out of those who voted for Mélenchon in the first round, only 42 per cent voted for Macron in the second, down from 52 per cent in 2017 (Lair 2022). The Macron régime has been revealed for what it always was, ideologically speaking: a political project of the right, favouring security and merit, and proposing hope instead of solidarity.

The future of France

There are competing visions for the future of France moving forward in 2022. With the continuation of the Macron régime going full swing following Macron's re-election, the prospect of a return to the old dichotomy between the traditional parties of the left and right seems improbable. The neoliberal right, now firmly behind Macron's second term in office, has an agenda of economic reforms which plan on strengthening the state as an arbiter of economic activity, while simultaneously reducing the role of the state in direct economic activity. More of what we have seen in 2017–22 is to be expected in the five years to come. In the first instance, a continuation of the *régime* for the state discussed in Chapter 1: a reduction in state spending in social areas and a strengthening of the sovereign functions of the state. The key reform is likely to be pensions, as the project for pension reform was put on hold during the COVID-19 pandemic, and Macron promised to push ahead with it during the elections in 2022. But other reforms may soon follow, building on the changes to unemployment benefits and reform of the labour code of Macron's first term. The blueprint for changes in the future remains the Attali Commission report of 2008, on which Macron laboured tirelessly. In addition to widespread shrinking of France's civil service, in desperate need of a diet, the report also calls for measures that Macron has not been able to tackle during his first term. The first, and most important of these, is a strengthening of the EU's stability and growth pact. The reduction of public deficits for Eurozone members is a real vote-winner on the right, where analogies of running the state like one runs a business are very popular. We will come back to this claim when analyzing the possibility of a New Left later in this conclusion, but for now it's enough to say that public austerity has won the argument of fiscal policy in France. A strong European position here is desired as this has the advantage of putting the blame for these policies, where they require intense and painful belt-tightening measures, on faceless bureaucrats in Brussels. The Norwegian television series *Occupied* (Lund and Skjoldbjaerg, 2015) offers a clear sense of this Brussels threat. In a fictional near future in which the US has withdrawn from NATO, Norway elects a green party to power which stops oil production in the country, before coming under quasi-occupation by Russian forces. But the villains in this drama are less the occupation forces than the bureaucrats in Brussels, who are the ones giving the Norwegian prime minister the ultimatum which triggers the occupation. Concerned with their own energy needs, other EU countries under the leadership of the European Commission organize the occupation, to benefit themselves. *Occupied*, which premiered in 2015, came after the most dramatic EU events that followed the 2010 financial crisis. In 2015, Greek negotiations with the Troika – the European Commission, the European Central Bank, and the International Monetary Fund – broke down, leading to a snap election which saw radical left leader Alexis Tsipras come to power. But before he could threaten the stability of the Eurozone with a vote on exiting the Eurozone, the European Union, or defaulting on the debt, Tsipras had to back down over the summer of 2015 – leading to the resignation of his finance minister Yanis Varoufakis. Less dramatic in reality than in fiction, pressure from the EU is nonetheless real – and has the advantage of shielding European leaders from putting these direct pressures on their allies. With a new Chancellor in Germany, himself highly favourable towards the strengthening of the stability and growth pact, one can expect Macron's second term in office to put pressure on the EU to enforce the rules ever so strictly, particularly after the relaxation of the rules during the COVID-19 pandemic, where they were essentially shelved to help governments deal with the economics of the pandemic and its lockdowns.

The France of the future, under the new Macron presidency, will also continue its quest to build up the muscle of its régime. With a considerable growth in police numbers between 2017 and 2022, and the consolidation of emergency powers into law, the first term of Macron's presidency has opened the path for a security state of ever-growing proportions. The COVID-19 pandemic has further enhanced this security state, with a particularly heavy-handed response by French authorities, compared to their European neighbours. With the virus now looking increasingly like an endemic-epidemic virus, akin to the outbreaks of smallpox studied by Foucault, the response by public authorities is likely to become more polarized and to differ increasingly between countries. If the response in France since 2020 is indicative of the future, we can expect a rise in the security apparatus around the response to COVID-19 as it becomes a part of our everyday lives. But the area of growth for the security state favoured by Macron is in the international sphere. Macron has shown that he is ready to extend France's projection of power overseas, challenging those he perceives to be against the liberal world order he favours. Whether it is a strong stance against Erdoğan's Turkey, pressure on the régimes of Orbán in Hungary, Morawiercki in Poland, or even Johnson in the UK, Macron has stood firm in public against the enemies of his version of liberalism. French troops are still committed to number of theatres in Western Africa, the Middle East and the Baltic states. Out of these, Operation Barkhane in the Sahel region is by far the largest, and despite Macron's lukewarm attitude to the armed forces, there is considerable room for a larger commitment of French forces overseas beyond 2022. Because France is unable to act independently in many theatres, this larger involvement is likely to depend heavily on US enthusiasm for intervention. Macron, unlike Chirac in 2003, would not oppose plans for US intervention, and would likely be a partner in a coalition of the willing. With the outbreak of war in Ukraine in February 2022, Macron largely positioned himself as a champion of the military expansion of Europe against the Russian threat. After negotiating with Putin days before the invasion, Macron attempted to impose himself as the dealmaker over the crisis, trying to broker a ceasefire unsuccessfully on numerous occasions. Playing the middle-ground position, in line with his philosophy of '*en même temps*', Macron tried to thread a thin line between the more belligerent rhetoric of his American (Borger 2022) and British (Scotto Di Santolo 2022) allies while still supporting Ukraine in its defensive war effort, and backing sanctions against Russia. With Germany announcing large investment in military spending over the next few years, as well as a shift in policy towards Russia, Macron's second term will have a unique opportunity to boost the other arm of the security régime he has already built internally. Macron had already started this process, and with a tense geopolitical situation in Eastern Europe and war in Ukraine it will likely take a priority role in the years to come.

France has been a meritocratic society for a long time, and Macron is a product of this society as much as a defender of it. His proposed reforms of his alma mater, ENA, are still unclear but they seem to aim towards a widening participation in the new institute that will take its place, merging with 13 other public service institutes in the country. There may be an appetite for a larger set of reforms of higher education in France, although confrontation with the student body is always a risky strategy for the executive. One can imagine that the current system, with tuition fees set at €170 a year for a bachelor's degree at most universities, would be a likely target for a liberalization programme *à la française*. There are already, after all, numerous private universities in France, including the one attended by Macron, Sciences Po Paris. At the moment of writing, the fees for this elite institution, delivering bachelor's and master's degrees, vary according to the candidate's family income, ranging from €0 to €13,000 a year. One can imagine such a system becoming generalized for all French public universities, providing a strong basis for a system of higher education based on merit. Macron's government has already initiated reforms of the higher education sector, enforcing selection at public universities – a practice hitherto limited to private institutions. The flip side of a merit system, as we have seen, is the sentiment it creates for those who have not reached the top of the meritocracy. Since merit makes one responsible for one's own fortune, the losers in a meritocracy – that is, the majority of the population – can respond extremely negatively to a defence of the system by those who have benefited from it. The *gilets jaunes*, without much doubt, were a direct reaction to meritocracy, as I argue in my book on the movement. It is impossible to predict what type of opposition may come from that direction in the future, nor which part of the population may participate, but suffice to say that the risk is as real over the coming future as it was in 2018 at the beginning of the movement. With grumblings coming from the armed forces and a history of unrest in the *banlieues*, the continued rise of the cost of living through additional energy costs and rising inflation, the social situation is shaky at best at the beginning of Macron's second mandate.

The death of the PS and LR

In the long term, a return to status quo ante, where political parties from the traditional right – let us call it the Gaullist right, which followed more closely the model of Bonapartism we discussed in Chapter 1 – and the socialist left remains a possibility but seems unlikely. The traditional right fared better electorally than the left in 2017, but that advantage has now disappeared in the 2022 presidential elections. The appeal of Macronism has been formidable among supporters of the traditional parties. There are still recalcitrant voices from the more conservative right, who oppose some of Macron's more socially liberal rhetoric, notably on family values, but generally the economic programme of neoliberalism with strong investment in the entrepreneurial spirit coupled with cuts to social spending suits the right-wing electorate rather well. The main difference between the new right and the old one, then, seems to be on social issues. The Gaullist right could come back with support from the Catholic bloc. But this Catholic bloc, even if not negligible in the recent history of the country, having mobilized against the law on same-sex marriage under Hollande, is hardly a majoritarian force within France. It is also squeezed, as we will see, from the extreme-right, which claims to take up some of its heritage. In 2022, Le Pen has gained large parts of the Catholic vote – although she still came second to Macron in the first round of the elections (Ipsos 2022). Those on the right who have rallied to Macron's movement have sensed that the battle between old right and new right is not worth having, that accommodation can be made and a future within the new movement is possible for them.

The traditional left, which took power in 1981, was led by the PS, which has since become a *persona non grata* in French politics. Whereas François Hollande won the presidency in 2012, Anne Hidalgo's campaign in 2022 could never get off the ground and she finished with just over 2 per cent of the vote in the first round of the elections. Part of the reason for this failure is that Macron has encroached on the terrain occupied by socialists since 1983, the party being socially liberal but economically supportive of neoliberalism. The choice, by socialists, to move their target electorate to the *bourgeois bloc* is widely documented, and is not unique to France. The trouble for the socialists is that this electorate is probably better served by Macron. Having abandoned the working classes, parties of the left, in France as in other European countries, have left the door open to others to cajole that electorate. With the fall of the French Communist Party, from capturing 20 per cent of the French electorate in 1979 to not even fielding candidates 30 years later in 2009, meant that this electorate was left for other parties to grab – but not the socialists. Mélenchon in France has been able to capture some of these voters, but it is also clear that many have been attracted by the far right. There is a distinct lack of vision for the future from those two traditional parties of the left, the socialists and the communists. Anne Hidalgo has been campaigning on a promise to reach carbon neutrality by 2050 – hardly a vote-winner among the working classes more concerned with the rising costs of energy than with how that energy is produced in the first place – and gender equality for pay. Those measures are ones likely to seduce the *bourgeois bloc* – environmentally conscious, concerned with gender equality – rather than the working classes. More of the same was the promise of the socialists, with the result that no one, not even Hidalgo's party members, believed in her prospects during the campaign (Belaïch 2021). A return to the old political changeover system, with the two main parties being either in power or the chief opposition party, seems unlikely at this stage. Both the Gaullist right and the socialists have largely lost the momentum that kept them in power or as the principle party of opposition. The new right under Macron has successfully captured part of the electorate, and if a new opposition emerges, it will have to find a niche outside of what is already on offer by the new powers.

The far right

The main opposition to Macron, if one is to believe his own rhetoric, is from the far right. Le Pen, Macron's adversary in 2017 and in 2022, was equally keen to portray her candidacy as the only alternative to Macron – and indeed to the established political parties that preceded his rise to power. Le Pen, who has campaigned on issues of security and immigration both in 2017 and 2022, proposes a vision of France for the future that is more homogeneous culturally – and racially – than the current multicultural and diverse reality of French cities. Since Macron has largely outflanked her on the security issue, leaving little for her to contribute in opposition, the debate has been around the role of immigration in French society and the place that Muslims can play in French society. The primary difference between the open-society vision of Macron and the closed-society vision of Le Pen is over immigration policy and Islam. On economic issues, the National Rally, Le Pen's rebranded party following the 2017 defeat in the second round of the presidential election, has nothing to propose to oppose Macron. There is no plan for a withdrawal from the Eurozone, or from the EU, in Le Pen's vision of the future. There is little to suggest an industrial strategy worthy of the name, not even one that favours French firms over others. The only difference between Macron and Le Pen, thus, is over hope and fear. Whereas Macron brands himself as the candidate of hope, Le Pen galvanizes French fears about *déclassement* – both political and industrial, fears about immigration, around the issue of the role of Islam in French society, and fears about a globalized world where French might can no longer be projected.

It is an open secret that the French armed forces largely favour the RN (Johannès 2021). Twice as likely to vote for the far right, the security forces have been increasingly vocal about their opposition to key policies and demanding increased involvement in political life. In the army, up to half of all those enlisted were planning to vote for Marine Le Pen ahead of the election. Marine Le Pen was keen to align herself with the 20 disgruntled generals that openly criticized Macron in a public letter, portrayed a vision of the future of France as one of civil war between the security services and the alliance of *islamo-gauchistes* – the supposed melting together of radical Islam and the left. In practice, there is little no evidence of an alliance between Islamists and the left, but the use of the term by members of Macron's government speaks volumes about their attempts to challenge the far right on its own ground (Louati 2021). Meanwhile, influential Youtubers of the far right have been increasing their presence and radicalizing the message to their ever-growing audience. Captivating a young, white, male audience, they are more openly accepting a fascist heritage, arming themselves and creating videos on 'how to kill a leftist', and growing support for seizing power in non-electoral ways (Gross 2021). The battle lines may be fanciful at this stage – the possibility of a military coup, or a militia-like rebellion seem blown out of proportion – but the rhetoric is here to create fear and the sensation of the urgency of action.

An analysis of what the Front National, and its heir the Rassemblement National have done in the cities they have won through the ballot-box is revealing for what is to be expected if it were ever to come to power. Out of the 11 cities won over by the Front National in 2014, four were run by new party members in their thirties, in an attempt to redress the image of the party which had been mired by financial scandals under Jean-Marie Le Pen's leadership. What these local authorities have in common is their reliance on austerity measures and lower local taxes in their financial organization of the budget. Austerity is the *modus vivendi* of the RN at the local level, as well as its reform plan for France at the national level. Savings in these *mairies* were achieved by cutting grants to local associations, reducing the numbers of municipal employers, or not replacing staff who leave. In addition to austerity, it is an obsession with security that has been the defining characteristic of the RN's political programme. More local police and more surveillance cameras have been the hallmarks of the local security régimes. Last but not least, it is over identity politics that the RN has distinguished itself in local politics. In Beaucaire, the mayor cancelled substitute menus for local schools (effectively targeting Muslim children's dietary requirements), cancelled 'oriental dance' shows and launched local 'anti-immigration charters' (Causit 2020). The de-demonization of the party has partly paid off, in that some local officials have managed to show they can answer the concerns of their citizens, but they merely reinforce the diagnostic at the national level: that the only significant point of difference with Macron's ideology is over immigration and Islam.

The left

If Macron's ideology, founded around the ideals of security, merit and hope, is the foundation of the new right, what could a left opposition look like beyond 2022? Mélenchon has been the candidate of the left after the socialist debacle which followed the presidency of Francois Hollande, a role confirmed in the 2022 presidential election where he was the third candidate, narrowly behind Marine Le Pen in the first round. His programme for the 2022 elections is telling of the alternative offered by his party *La France Insoumise* (LFI). Based around four themes, namely democracy, ecology, social progress and independence, LFI offered an alternative to Macron's programme. Mélenchon, however, is not a figure behind which the rest of the left has been able to galvanize support, and there are other movements on the left including the greens and various offshoots of the Socialist Party such as Benoît Hamon that made a bid in the 2017 elections. Even the very far left, personified by the Trostkyist Poutou in 2017 and 2022, managed to score points during presidential debates (although this did not translate into large electoral support). Poutou struck a chord then when he attacked Le

Pen for not representing the working class. As Mondon (2020, 17) points out, only one in every ten workers votes for the far right – as even through a third of votes went to Le Pen's party, abstention among this group was nearly two out of three. It was the great failure of Mélenchon in 2017 not to have been able to capture more of the working-class vote that did not go to Le Pen, not to have motivated workers to come out to vote, not to have capitalized on the void left by the retreating Socialist Party.

If the left is ever to come to power again, it will have to have a convincing answer to the new right embodied by the Macron régime. It will have to answer the ideology of the new right, the belief in and defence of the core values of security, merit, and hope – for example by defending an alternative to this ideology. What better place to start than by defending the opposing values to those of the new right? Against security, safety; against merit, democracy; against hope, solidarity. Let me illustrate the possibility of this new left, founded on an ideology distinct from the one in power, with three examples of how these core values can be defended as a programme for the future. These are merely reactions here, and of course a new left will not only react but also have power of initiative, proposing its own values rather than attacking those of its opponents. But a negation is a good place to start, and for our purposes here it will serve to show how a left opposition to Macron is possible.

Against the growing security state defended by Macron, as we have seen in Chapter 2, the growth of a safety-providing state is possible. Many will share the view that the current arrangements in France are unduly corporatist, protecting the interests of a few over the interests of all. One does not need to agree with the growth of the security state to accept that some of the *acquis* it is challenging are worth looking at. A change in the labour code, a reform of pensions, and fairer unemployment benefits are all possible without the rise in the security state as has happened under Macron. One measure that can act as a catalyst for this change is universal basic income (UBI). Although support for UBI is not exclusive to the left of the political spectrum, and not universal within the left (Schwander 2020), it has the potential of mobilizing people behind a common system of safety which could work for all in society. UBI has many intuitive appeals – it is universal, thereby not based on individual merit; it is basic, reflecting the most common acceptable standard of living in a society; it provides a clear income, ensuring safe and reliable means for survival for all. Its implementation would be a monumental change in social and economic relations. UBI, according to Bidadanure (2019), has a long and complicated history that cuts across the ideological divide. Being a form of welfare state proposal, it originates, however, in social democratic thinking, with key influences being Thomas Paine in the eighteenth century, Joseph Charlier in the nineteenth century, and Martin Luther King Jr. in the twentieth century. But it has also been defended by some on the neoliberal right, most notably Milton Friedman, as a way to reduce state bureaucracy. Dismissed by some on the left precisely on those grounds – that it is suspiciously too libertarian in outlook – it nonetheless proposes a safety system that has five key advantages, according to Bidadanure. In the first instance, it is a cash payment, as opposed to an in-kind benefit. This has the advantage of giving flexibility to the recipient, in this case all eligible citizens who would benefit from it. Unlike food stamps or housing benefits, all can equally use the cash as they see fit. In the second instance, it is individual. By granting all eligible citizens UBI, it does away with household biases that particularly affect women. Third, it is unconditional rather than conditional. Unlike benefit schemes that assume recipients want to cheat the system and therefore have to justify their claims, the unconditional nature of UBI does away with the linking of the right to an income with the obligation of work. It is also universal, as the name suggests. From the richest person in society to the poorest, all would equally be able to claim UBI. Of course, the fiscal implications mean that this income would then be taxed back from those at the top of the earning pyramid. But the appeal of universal systems cannot be underestimated – if all share equally in the benefits, regardless of whether they end up forming 100 per cent of their income or 0 per cent, the simplicity of the scheme fosters support. Fifth, it is regular and provides real and concrete safety for all. Unlike other payments, that are conditional, one-off, or temporary, UBI creates a definite safety net for all in society. Benoît Hamon in 2017 campaigned on a UBI platform and, although his candidacy failed to galvanize support, UBI has been firmly established as a proposal of the left in French politics.

Against the rising tide of merit, where those who work hard get the benefits they deserve – and the lazy suffer what they must – the revolutionary spirit has defended a model of citizenship based on equality defined in more universal terms. It was the genius of François Mitterrand (2010) to publish in 1964 his *Le Coup d'État permanent* as a critique of the constitution of the Fifth Republic, and a betrayal of de Gaulle's promises of 1958. Although calls for a Sixth Republic in France are controversial, and there is little support for a full revision of the constitution, paradoxically there is also support for a democratization of institutions. The Fifth Republic has given many powers to the president, but also to the government through the powers of the prime minister. It has made a mockery of the democratic process, as parliament – supposedly the ultimate guarantee of democratic representation – can be (and has been) bypassed completely by the executive. The state has also been increasingly technocratized, and many decisions have now been delegated to unelected officials such as the prefects. It is not only the *énarques*, the elite administrators of France, but also the plethora of officials making important, controversial and ultimately political decisions despite never having run for office. It is telling that Macron's first election was to the highest office in the land. This concentration of power in the hands of unelected officials is favoured by the Macron régime that has accelerated its process rather than slowed it down. The flip side of this ideological position is, of course, that espoused by the *gilets jaunes* during their year-and-a-half of weekly protests. A direct reaction to the technocratization of everday life, the *gilets jaunes* gathered around the RIC, the citizen-initiated referendum. Instead of technocratic control: direct democracy; instead of *énarques*: referenda; instead of elections: participation. A programme for a Sixth Republic may not be on the agenda today, but reforms to the democratic process would be a way for the left to take into account popular demands. As I have argued in my book on the *gilets jaunes*, (Devellennes 2021) the importance here is to think about who has the initiative. The key feature of the RIC is not that it is a referendum *per se*, but that it allows for popular initiative to shape public debates. Referenda have their faults, but initiative is a popular demand that can be actualized in various constitutional ways. Beyond the referendum, one could consider a right to recall elected officials (the slogan *Macron Démission* [Macron, resign] was widespread during the *gilets jaunes* demonstrations), the ability to revise, periodically, constitutional arrangements through citizen conventions (Chile is, at the time of writing, undergoing such a process), and the importance of local decision-making in what is highly centralized state are all alternatives that have widespread appeal as democratic features.

Finally, set against hope, the value of solidarity provides a much more solid affective basis for the left. Disappointed hope, we have seen, all too often leads to despair. No political orientation should know this better than the left. Old communists, in France, all too often shifted to the Front National after 1991 and the disappointment of their hope of a world revolution. The promises of the *lendemain du grand soir*, of a future for the world shaped by revolution and socialism, have caused those for whom these hopes were crushed to despair. Against hope, thus, a stronger and more stable emotion can act on a political basis. What could be better than solidarity, an affective bond between those who are suffering, those who are affected by the destructions of neoliberalism, those who are on the receiving end of rising inequalities? Specific policies can address this issue of solidarity, but its affective potential also needs to be embodied by leaders on the left. Just as Macron can motivate a crowd while opening a high-tech campus in a former train station in Paris, a candidate of the left should be able to motivate a crowd of *gilets jaunes*, an assembly of striking workers, or a rally on a May Day demonstration. Against a régime that has violently repressed workers on their celebration of solidarity on 1 May, against a president who stood behind his adviser who impersonated a police office to beat up May Day protesters, against a government that has pushed for repression of a popular movement leading to deaths, hundreds of injuries and bodily mutilations on the side of demonstrators, it should be easy to find a figure to unite the opposition on the left. Only those who show an affinity for political emotions, particularly emotions of solidarity and support, can replace hope with a positive political emotion. Gilles Perret and François Ruffin's film, *J'veux du Soleil* (Perret and Ruffin 2019) illustrates this affective dimension of politics. A member of parliament for *La France Insoumise*, Ruffin – who went to the same school as Macron, the Jesuit *La Pro'* in Amiens – is perhaps the only politician who managed to get widespread support from those participating in the social movement. In the film, where Ruffin is filmed by Perret as they tour the roundabouts of France where the *gilets jaunes* congregate and interview the participants, an affective bond is clearly created between the politician and the demonstrators. If Hidalgo, the socialist candidate, Mélenchon, the LFI candidate, or Jadot, the green candidate, had been able to draw on this affective dimension, they would have done the emotional labour necessary for a left victory.

Ruffin (Laïreche 2022) was also one of the few voices to identify the failure of his own party, LFI, in the first round of the 2022 presidential elections, as a failure to mobilize the working classes. Behind the fact that two of France's most precarious socioeconomic categories, the *ouvriers* and *employés* (blue-collar and lower-paid white-collar workers) preferred Le Pen over Mélenchon, this outcome obfuscates the fact that most voters from these two categories actually do not vote at all. Abstention and spoiled ballots are extremely high among blue-collar workers (Ipsos 2022), almost as high as abstention among the unemployed (33 per cent for former, 35 per cent for the latter). For all its pretentions to represent ordinary workers, LFI has largely replicated the social structure of the Socialist Party – its members are highly educated, urban-based, and there are still no blue-collar workers among its elected members in the National Assembly. The challenge to come, for the left in France, remains to see if they can incorporate the material needs and preferences of the French working classes, and fully integrate them within their ranks. This seems to be an uphill battle, and one for which the existing parties are ill equipped. The material demands of the working classes, namely full employment and rising standards of living, are at odds with other goals of the left, namely a balancing of budgets under austerity measures, and an ecological transition which would hurt lowest-earners the most. There are options open to the left to address those challenges, the question being whether the left will manage to unite behind a common programme to promote those goals. Modern Monetary Theory has notably proven popular in promoting a full-employment strategy (Kelton 2020), but this necessitates a coordination between fiscal and monetary policy that will revive old tensions in the left between pro-EU advocates and Eurosceptics. Mélenchon's split with the PS came after the pro-EU faction won over leadership of the PS after the failed referendum for a constitution for Europe in 2005, with Mélenchon taking many of the EU critics with him in the transition. A shift to more ecologically friendly energy use is also fraught with tensions within the left, between advocates of nuclear energy and those favouring a shift to renewables, the only major policy disagreement between Mélenchon and his former communist allies in 2022. The legislative elections of June 2022, which are due to happen after the time of writing, will have been a first test of the left's ability to unite despite their differences. If the left manages to put together a serious challenge and gain seats in the National Assembly, it could be in a position to oppose Macron's reforms until 2027. In the event of an outright majority of the left in the legislature, an effective opposition could take place. But past elections have always given the president a majority, so this outcome seemed unlikely in April 2022. Even a strong showing for the left could build momentum ahead of 2027, and help to frame the debate over the course of the presidency. Yet, without a reliable strategy to win over working-class voters and address their concerns, these scenarios still look doomed to failure. A profound and deep reform of left-wing politics is the only answer to Macron's second term. The left knows what to do, it remains to be seen if it can unite, mobilize and win over the next five years.

References

Agamben, G. (2005) *State of Exception*. Chicago: University of Chicago Press.

Agnew, H. (2017) 'Emmanuel Macron thinks big in vision for French tech unicorns', *Financial Times*, 20 August.

Allard-Huver, F. and Escurignan, J. (2018) '*Black Mirror*'s Nosedive as a new Panopticon: Interveillance and digital parrhesia in alternative realities' in Cirucci, A. and Vacker, B. (eds) *Black Mirror and Critical Media Theory*, Lanham: Rowman & Littlefield Publishing Group, pp. 43–54.

Amable, B. and Palombarini, S. (2021) *The Last Neoliberal: Macron and the Origins of France's Political Crisis*. London: Verso.

Ambler, J. (1991) 'Ideas, interests, and the French welfare state' in Ambler, J. (ed) *The French Welfare State*. New York: New York University Press, pp. 1–28.

Arnault, B. (2017) 'Pourquoi je vote Emmanuel Macron', *Les Échos,* 5 May.

Arneson, R. (2018) 'Dworkin and luck egalitarianism: A comparison' in Olsaretti, S. (ed) *The Oxford Handbook of Distributive Justice*. Oxford: Oxford University Press.

Attali, J. (2008) *Rapport de la Commission pour la libération de la croissance Française*. Paris: XO Éditions.

Aussilloux, V., Frocrain, P., Harfi, M., Lallement, R., Tabarly, G., Beeker, E., Giorgi, D. and Meilhan, N. (2020) 'Les politiques industrielles en France. Évolutions et comparaisons internationales', *France Stratégie*, report for the National Assembly. Available from: https://www.strategie.gouv.fr/publications/politiques-industrielles-france-evolutions-comparaisons-internationales.

Beaune, C. (2020) 'Europe beyond COVID-19', *Politique étrangère*, Vol. 85, No. 3: 9–29.

Belaïch, C. (2021) 'Plongée dans la campagne d'Anne Hidalgo: «Il y a une sorte de fatalisme, personne ou presque ne croit à la présidentielle»', *Libération,* 25 November.

Bell, D. (2014) 'What is liberalism?', *Political Theory,* Vol. 42, No. 6: 682–715.

Berdah, A. (2020) 'Macron lance la dernière étape de son «spoil system»', *Le Figaro*, 30 July.

Berlin, I. (1969) *Four Essays on Liberty*. Oxford: Oxford University Press.

Bickerton, C. (2022) 'How to boil a brog (2) ft. Chris Bickerton', *aufhebunga bunga*. Available from: https://bungacast.com/2022/04/20/257-how-to-boil-a-frog-2-ft-chris-bickerton/

Bickerton, C. and Invernizzi Accetti, C. (2021) *Technopopulism: The New Logic of Democratic Politics*. Oxford: Oxford University Press.

Bidadanure, J. (2019) 'The political theory of Basic Income', *Annual Review of Political Science*, Vol. 22: 481–501.

Blavignat, Y. (2018) 'L'affaire des «foulards de Creil»: la République laïque face au voile islamique', *Le Figaro*, 27 July.

Bloch, E. (1995) *The Principle of Hope*. Cambridge, MA: MIT Press.

Borger, J. (2022) 'Macron declines to follow Biden and call Russian acts in Ukraine "genocide"', *The Guardian*, 13 April.

Bourgeois, J.-G. and Vichard, T. (2019) 'Macron lui avait dit de «traverser la rue pour trouver du travail»: un an après, qu'est-il devenu?', *Europe 1*, 22 September.

Brooker, C. (2016) 'Nosedive', *Black Mirror* [TV series].

Budgen, S. (2022) 'Shrewd Tortoise', *New Left Review*, 21 April.

Carrat, F., Figoni, J., Henny, J., Desenclos, J.-C., Kab, S., de Lamballerie, X. and Zins, N. (2021) 'Evidence of early circulation of SARS-CoV-2 in France: findings from the population-based "CONSTANCES" cohort', *European Journal of Epidemiology*, Vol. 36: 219–22.

Carriat, J. (2020) 'Emmanuel Macron forme des «vœux d'espoir» pour 2021', *Le Monde*, 31 December.

Causit, C. (2020) 'Municipales 2020: comment le Rassemblement National a géré les villes conquises en 2014', *franceinfo*, 11 February.

Centre d'observation de la société (2020) 'Le chômage de longue durée se stabilise enfin', 19 March. Available from: http://www.observationsociete.fr/travail/evol-chomage-longue-duree.html

Challier, R. (2017) 'Les paradoxes de la dédiabolisation du FN', *métropolitiques*, 10 April.

Chomsky, N. (2017) *Requiem for the American Dream*. New York: Seven Stories Press.

Colin, N. (2018) '«Un pognon de dingue»: Macron a 30 ans de retard', *L'Obs*, 28 June.

Comte, K. (2021) '«La tolérance, c'est zéro»: les contrôles renforcés à l'heure du couvre-feu', *franceinfo*, 1 February.

Comte-Sponville, A. (2008) *The Little Book of Atheist Spirituality*. London: Penguin.

Comte-Sponville, A. (2011) *Traité du désespoir et de la béatitude*. Paris: Presses Universitaires de France.

Cossardeaux, J. (2020) 'Coronavirus: policiers et gendarmes sous haute pression sanitaire', *Les Echos*, 17 March.

Devellennes, C. (2021) *The Gilets Jaunes and the New Social Contract*. Bristol: Bristol University Press.

Droit-finances.net (2021) 'Réforme de l'assurance chômage 2021 (réforme Macron)'. Available from: https://droit-finances.commentcamarche.com/salaries/guide-salaries/1559-reforme-de-l-assurance-chomage-2021-reforme-macron/

Duverger, M. (1977) *La monarchie républicaine*. Paris: Robert Laffont.

Dworkin, R. (1981a) 'What is equality? Part 1: Equality of welfare', *Philosophy and Public Affairs*, Vol. 10, No. 3: 185–246.

Dworkin, R. (1981b) 'What is equality? Part 2: Equality of resources', *Philosophy and Public Affairs*, Vol. 10, No. 4: 283–345.

Dworkin, R. (2000) *Sovereign Virtue: The Theory and Practice of Equality*. Cambridge, MA: Harvard University Press.

Élysée (2021) 'Vœux 2022 aux Français', 31 December.

Élysée (2022) 'Adresse aux Français', 2 March.

Erforth, B. (2020) *Contemporary French Security Policy in Africa: On Ideas and Wars*. London: Palgrave Macmillan.

Fabre-Bernadac, J.-P. (2021) '«Pour un retour de l'honneur de nos gouvernants»: 20 généraux appellent Macron à défendre le patriotisme', *Valeurs Actuelles*, 21 April.

Fazi, T. (2022) 'The Left should not vote for Macron', *UnHeard*, 22 April.

Femme Actuelle (2020) 'Emmanuel Macron: découvrez quel est son vin préféré', 23 July.

Forbes (2021) 'Comment Bernard Arnault est devenu, quelques heures, l'homme le plus riche du monde!', 2 August.

Foucault, M. (2009) *Security, Territory, Population: Lectures at the Collège de France 1977–78*. London: Palgrave Macmillan.

France 24 (2020) 'Emmanuel Macron présente ses vœux aux Français: «L'espoir est là, dans ce vaccin»', YouTube. Available from: https://www.youtube.com/watch?v=xjQJuJWLi4k&ab_channel=FRANCE24

France Inter (2022) Tweet of 22 April. Available from: https://twitter.com/franceinter/status/1517390208907591680?s=20&t=HpGL79vwLIhg2dx0nrDzrw

Frank, D. and McPhail, M. (2005) 'Barack Obama's address to the 2004 Democratic National Convention: Trauma, compromise, consilience, and the (im)possibility of racial reconciliation', *Rhetoric and Public Affairs*, Vol. 8, No. 4: 571–93.

Fukuyama, F. (1992) *The End of History and the Last Man*. New York: Free Press.

Gadamer, H.-G. (2004) *Truth and Method*. 2nd revised edition. London: Continuum.

Gamble, A. (1988) *The Free Economy and the Strong State*. London: Palgrave Macmillan.

Geoghegan, V. (2008) 'Pandora's box: Reflections on a myth', *Critical Horizons*, Vol. 9, No. 1: 24–41.

Giles, C. (2021) 'IMF proposes "solidarity" tax on pandemic winners and wealthy,' *Financial Times*, 7 April.

Gross, A. (2021) 'France's online "fascist-sphere" feeds rightwing electoral hopes', *Financial Times*, 25 August.

Gugelot, F. (2017) 'Interrogation sur le devenir du catholicisme en France, entre minorité et marginalité', *Revue d'histoire du protestantisme*, Vol. 2, No. 4: 561–72.

Hansen, L. (2006) *Security as Practice: Discourse Analysis and the Bosnian War*. London: Routledge.

Hochuli, A., Hoare, A. and Cunliffe, P. (2021) *The End of the End of History: Politics in the Twenty-First Century*. Winchester: Zero Books.

Holbach, P.-H.T. d' (1999) *Système de la Nature*, in Holbach, P.-H.T. d', *Œuvres Philosophiques, Tome II*, ed Jackson, J.-P., Paris: Coda.

Honneth, A. (1992) *The Struggle for Recognition: The Moral Grammar of Social Conflicts*. Cambridge, MA: MIT Press.

Humphrys, S. (2006) 'Legalizing lawlessness: On Giorgio Agamben's State of Exception', *The European Journal of International Law*, Vol. 17, No. 3: pp. 677–87.

Insee (Institut national de la statistique et des études économiques) (2021) 'Au premier trimestre 2021, le taux de chômage est quasi stable à 8,1 %', 29 June. Available from: https://www.insee.fr/fr/statistiques/5400024

Ipsos (2017) '1er tour sociologie des électorats et profils des abstentionistes', 23 April. Available from: https://www.ipsos.com/sites/default/files/files-fr-fr/doc_associe/ipsos-sopra-steria_sociologie-des-electorats_23-avril-2017-21h.pdf

Ipsos (2022) 'Sociologie des électorats et profils des abstentionistes', 10 April. Available from: https://www.ipsos.com/sites/default/files/ct/news/documents/2022-04/Ipsos%20Sopra%20Steria_Sociologie%20des%20e%CC%81lectorats_10%20Avril%2020h30.pdf

Jacob, E. (2018) 'Affaire Benalla: ce qu'il faut retenir de l'audition de Michel Delpuech à l'Assemblée', *Le Figaro*, 23 July.

Johannès, F. (2021) 'Quatre militaires sur dix votent pour l'extrême droite', *Le Monde*, 30 April.

John Paul II (1994) *Crossing the Threshold of Hope*. New York: Knopf Publishing Group.

Kelton, S. (2020) *The Deficit Myth: Modern Monetary Theory and the Birth of the People's Economy*. London: John Murray.

Kennedy, E. (1979) '"Ideology" from Destutt de Tracy to Karl Marx', *Journal of the History of Ideas*, Vol. 40, No. 3: 353–68.

Khemilat, F. (2021) 'France's new "separatism" law stigmatizes minorities and could backfire badly', *The Conversation*, 15 August.

La Sécurité Sociale (2021) 'Baromètre 2020 «Les Français et la Sécu»', 6 May.
Lair, N. (2022) 'Second tour: pour qui ont voté les électeurs de Mélenchon, Jadot, Pécresse, Zemmour ...', 24 April.
Laïreche, R. (2022) 'François Ruffin: «Jusqu'ici, nous ne parvenons pas à muer en espoir la colère des "fâchés pas fachos"»', *Libération*, 13 April.
Lamm, P. (2007) 'LVMH, un empire du luxe construit en vingt ans', *Les Échos*, 22 June.
Lang, D. (2022) 'Les programmes de Macron et Le Pen bénéficient tous les deux aux plus riches', *Quartier Général*, 18 April.
Laurence, J. (2021) 'Loi séparatisme: « On désarme spirituellement l'islam en France à un moment peu propice »', *La Croix*, 23 July.
Laurent, S. (2013) 'Derrière la grande illusion de la «Manif pour tous»', *Le Monde*, 31 March.
Le Figaro (2021) 'Le budget du ministère de l'Intérieur va augmenter de plus de 900 millions d'euros en 2022', 26 July.
Le Figaro (2022) '«Banque des parrainages»: Bayrou assure disposer d'une réserve suffisante pour que Le Pen et Zemmour concourent', 25 February.
Le Monde (2021) 'La dette publique de la France a atteint «son niveau le plus élevé depuis 1949»', 26 March.
Le Parisien (2018) 'Macron à un jeune chômeur: «Je traverse la rue et je vous trouve un emploi»', 16 September.
Le Point (2017) 'Emmanuel Macron: «Je ne céderai rien, ni aux fainéants, ni aux cyniques, ni aux extrêmes»', 8 September.
Le Scan Politique (2017) 'Emmanuel Macron évoque les «gens qui ne sont rien» et suscite les critiques', *Le Figaro*, 2 July.
Leboucq, F. (2021) 'Le projet «opération Ronces», visant à faire intervenir l'armée dans les banlieues, est-il une réalité?', *Libération*, 12 May.
Lemarié, A. (2021) 'Comment l'entourage d'Emmanuel Macron met en scène un président qui serait devenu épidémiologiste', *Le Monde*, 30 March.
Les Décodeurs (2018) 'Non, la fin de l'ISF ne fera pas économiser 500 millions d'euros à Bernard Arnault', *Le Monde*, 3 March.
Llorca, R. (2021) *La Marque Macron. Désillusions du Neutre*. Paris: Éditions de l'aube.
Lock, F. (2008a) *Edmund Burke, Volume I: 1730–1784*. Oxford: Oxford University Press.
Lock, F. (2008b) *Edmund Burke, Volume II: 1784–1797*. Oxford: Oxford University Press.
Louati, Y. (2021) 'What does Islamo-Gauchisme mean for the future of france and democracy?', *Berkley Center for Religion, Peace & World Affairs*. Available from: https://berkleycenter.georgetown.edu/responses/what-does-islamo-gauchisme-mean-for-the-future-of-france-and-democracy
Lund, K. and Skjoldbjærg, E. (2015) *Occupied* [TV series].
Machiavelli, N. (2003) *The Prince*. London: Penguin Classics.

Macron, E. (2016) *Révolution*. Saint-Amand-Montrond: XO Éditions.

Macron, E. (2017) 'Tweet message', Twitter, 4 May. Available from: https://twitter.com/emmanuelmacron/status/860111061340610561?lang=en

Magazine Marianne (2020) 'Emmanuel Macron annonce l'interdiction des déplacements non essentiels dès mardi midi', 17 March.

Majumdar, M. (2020) 'France and the world. The African dimension', in M. Demossier, D. Less, A. Mondon and N. Parish (eds) *The Routledge Handbook of French Politics and Culture*. London: Routledge.

Ministère de l'Intérieur (2018) 'Communiqué de presse', 28 September.

Ministère des Armées (2017) 'Revue Stratégique de Défense et de Sécurité Nationale', Bureau des Editions, October.

Mitterrand, F. (2010) *Le Coup d'état permanent*. Paris: Les Belles Lettres.

Mondon, A. (2020) 'From despair, to hope, to limbo. The French elections and the future of the Republic', in M. Demossier, D. Less, A. Mondon and N. Parish (eds) *The Routledge Handbook of French Politics and Culture*. London: Routledge.

Mondon, A. (2021) 'France's far right is setting the agenda because the mainstream allows it to', *Jacobin*, 4 October.

Mondon, A. and Winter, A. (2020) *Reactionary Democracy. How Racism and the Populist Far Right Became Mainstream*. London: Verso Books.

Morosi, M.-C. (2019) 'Le règne du style «En même temps» à l'Élysée', *Le Point*, 28 November.

Muxel, A. (2020) 'Youth and politics in France. Democratic deficit or new model of citizenship?', in M. Demossier, D. Less, A. Mondon and N. Parish (eds) (eds) *The Routledge Handbook of French Politics and Culture*. London: Routledge.

Nicolas, A. (2022) 'Sandrine Rousseau face à Fabien Roussel: comment la viande est devenue politique', *Philosophie magazine*, 9 February.

Nietzsche, F. (2001) *Beyond Good and Evil*. Cambridge: Cambridge University Press. (Original work published 1886.)

Nozick, R. (2001) *Anarchy, State, and Utopia*. Hoboken, NJ: L Wiley-Blackwell. (Original work published 1974.)

Obama, B. (2008) *The Audacity of Hope: Thoughts on Reclaiming the American Dream*. Edinburgh: Canongate.

Ollion, E. (2007) 'Le massacre contre le putsch – entretien avec Alain Dewerpe', *Vacarme*, 21 June.

Opinionway (2019) '2017–2019: la transformation politique du vote Macron', Available from: https://www.opinion-way.com/images/sondage-opinion/Le_Figaro_-_Analyse_B._Jeanbart_-_Nouvelle_composition_politique_du_vote_LREM_-_4_juin_2019.pdf

Orwell, G. (2000) *Nineteen Eighty-Four*. London: Penguin Classics.

Paglia, C. (1994) 'Pope Fiction. The pontiff's best-selling pontification', *The New Republic*, 26 December.

Pedder, S. (2018) *Révolution Française: Emmanuel Macron and the Quest to Reinvent a Nation*. London: Bloomsbury Continuum.
Perret, G. and Ruffin, F. (2019) *J'veux du Soleil*.
Phelan, S. (2014) *Neoliberalism, Media and the Political*. London: Palgrave Macmillan.
Phillips, J. (2006) 'Agencement/Assemblage', *Theory, Culture & Society*, Vol. 23, No. 2–3: 108–109.
Piketty, T. (2013) *Le Capital au XXIe siècle*. Paris: Seuil.
Plato (2007) *The Republic*. London: Penguin Books.
Plowright, A. (2017) *The French Exception: Emmanuel Macron – The Extraordinary Rise and Risk*. London: Icon Books Ltd.
Poncet, G. (2019) 'Gilets jaunes: malaise chez les militaires après l'annonce de Macron', *Le Point*, 21 March.
Popper, K. (1966) *The Open Society and Its Enemies, Vol. 1*, 5th edn. Princeton: Princeton University Press.
Public Sénat (2021) 'Séparatisme: le Sénat vote l'ensemble du texte après l'avoir fortement durci'. Available from: https://www.publicsenat.fr/article/parlementaire/separatisme-le-senat-vote-l-ensemble-du-texte-apres-l-avoir-fortement-durci
Quinault-Maupoil T. (2017) 'Débat: Le Pen et Macron s'écharpent sur le burkini', *Le Figaro*, 20 March.
Rawls, J. (1971) *A Theory of Justice*. Cambridge, MA: Harvard University Press.
Rémond, R. (1982) *Les Droites en France*. Paris: Aubier-Montaigne.
Ricotta, J. (2020) 'Ce que l'on sait de la vidéo d'un producteur tabassé par des policiers', *Europe 1*, 26 November.
Sandel, M. (2020) *The Tyranny of Merit: What's Become of the Common Good?* London: Allen Lane.
Schwander, H. (2020) 'The Left and universal basic income: The role of ideology in individual support', *Journal of International and Comparative Social Policy*, Vol. 36, Special issue 3: 237–68.
Scotto Di Santolo, A. (2022) 'Macron blocks Boris on sending tanks to Ukraine as NATO tensions surge over "red line"', *Express*, 25 March.
Séchan, R. (1975) *Amoureux de Paname*. Polydor.
Simpson, J. (2004) *Touching the Void*. New York: Perennial.
Sorkin, A., Well, J., Schlamme, T., Well, L., Attie, E., Cahn, D., et al (2006) *The West Wing: The Complete Series*. Warner Home Video.
Spinoza, B. (2003 [1677]) *Ethics*. Project Gutenberg. Available from: https://www.gutenberg.org/ebooks/3800
Syndicat des Avocats de France (2020) 'Mesure de confinement: les contrôles de police ne doivent être ni abusifs ni violents ni discriminatoires', 27 March.
Tresca, M. (2017) 'Le vote des catholiques: «François Fillon défend les valeurs familiales que je porte», dit Armelle', *La Croix*, 21 April.
Valeurs Actuelles (2021) '[Exclusif] Signez la nouvelle tribune des militaires', 11 May.

Vilars, T. (2021) '«Il lit toutes les études»: quand la macronie en fait des tonnes sur le président-épidémiologiste', *L'Obs*, 24 February.

Vincent, C. (2021) 'Révision du budget des armées: consultation a minima du Parlement par le gouvernement', *Le Monde*, 23 June.

Weber, M. (2005) *The Protestant Ethic and the Spirit of Capitalism*. London: Routledge. (Original work published 1905.)

Weil, P. (2009) 'Why the French laïcité is liberal', *Cardozo Law Review*, Vol. 30, No. 6: 2699–714.

White, S. (2022) 'Mélenchon the kingmaker: Macron and Le Pen count on far-left votes in battle for French presidency', *Financial Times*, 12 April.

World Inequality Database (2021) 'France'. Available from: https://wid.world/country/france/

Index

A

Abeille, Louis Paul 42–43
Accetti, Carlo Invernizzi 74–76
Afghanistan 89
Agamben, Giorgio 47–48
agape 93–94
agencement (assemblage) 1
Algeria 31, 46
Algiers putsch of 1961 46
Amable, Bruno 12, 19, 33, 34
Amiens 3, 111
ancien régime 25, 27, 40, 52, 93
antisemitism 99
army 31, 32, 41, 47, 55
   budget 21, 57–58
   doctrine 56–57
   expansion of 40, 103
   far right 106
   gilets jaunes 58
   open letters 58
Arnault, Bernard 83–85
Arthaud, Nathalie 97
assemblage 1, 16
ataraxia 80
Attali Commission 4, 18–19, 101
Attlee, Clement 70
austerity policies 5, 18–24, 35, 65, 94, 107
   see also liberalism; neoliberalism; welfare
Ayatollah Khomeini 89

B

banlieues 15, 58, 82, 104
Barthes, Roland 48–49
Bayrou, François 7, 100
Beaune, Clément 55
Bell, Duncan 31–32
Benalla affair 50–51
Bentham, Jeremy 41
Berlin, Isaiah 15
Bickerton, Christopher 74–76, 100
Bidadanure, Juliana Uhuru 108, 109
Black Mirror 41
   see also Brooker, Charlie

Blair, Tony 23, 33, 49, 85
Bloch, Ernst 87–88, 94
Boas, George 78
   see also hope
Bonapartism 17, 24, 26–27, 104
   see also Orléanist right; nationalist right; new right; right-wing politics in France, ultra right
bourgeois bloc 101
   benefits of 38
   centre left and 12, 105
   definition of 34
   Parti Socialiste and 29, 34
   support for president Macron 96
   see also Parti Socialiste
Brabeck, Peter 19
   see also Nestlé
Brexit referendum 9
Brooker, Charlie 41
Brussels threat 102
Burke, Edmund 2, 92–93
Burkina Faso 56
Bush, George W. 23, 61, 89

C

calling 16, 60, 65–67
   see also Luther, Martin
Calvin, John 67–68
caritas 93–94
   see also charity; Christian theology
Castaner, Christophe 58
Castex, Jean 8
Catherine the Great 93
Catholic Church 90–92
Catholicism 66, 88, 91
Catholic right 10
Catholics 89, 91, 104
causa sui 71
   see also Nietzsche, Friedrich
centre-left, politics of 12
Chad 56
charity 91–94
   see also caritas
Charlie Hebdo 91

Chile 110
China 22, 44, 46, 55
Chirac, Jacques 8, 28, 29
Chomsky, Noam 35
Christianity 60, 71–72, 78
Christian theology 79, 80, 86, 93
  see also caritas
Clinton, Bill 33, 49
closed society 10–11, 55
  see also open society
Clovis I 27, 92
Comte-Sponville, André 46, 80, 82, 94
  see also hope
conservatism 2
Constitution of France 7
contextualism 13, 30
Convention Citoyenne pour le Climat 75
Corbyn, Jeremy
couscousgate 97
COVID-19 59, 100
  hope and 81, 86
  neoliberal doctrine and 18, 36–38, 72
  public spending and 5, 54, 101
  response to 33, 65
  security policies and 16, 43–48, 51, 53, 55, 102–103
  vaccine for 37, 46
  see also hope; neoliberalism, security apparatus

D

d'Alembert, Jean le Rond 93
Darmanin, Gérald 98
de Beauvoir, Simone 82
de Bonald 25
déclassement 13, 83, 106
de Gaulle, Charles 7, 49, 97, 109
Delpuech, Michel 50
Democratic Party 12
Depardieu, Gérard 85
désespoir 80
  see also hope
Devellennes, Charles 61, 110
d'Holbach, P.H.T. 52, 93
Diderot, Denis 93
dirigisme (economic doctrine of strong state control) 2
discourse analysis 13, 14–15
Dupont-Aignan, Nicolas 99
Duverger, Maurice 28
Dworkin, Ronald 16
  luck egalitarianism 60, 63–65
dystopia 15, 41, 88, 94

E

École National d'Administration (ENA) 7–8, 18, 60, 66, 74, 75, 103
Edict of Nantes 88
Elizabethan Poor Law 92–93
Élysée Palace 19, 27, 98

Encyclopédie 93
  see also d'Alembert, Jean le Rond; Diderot, Denis
end of history 6–7
  see also Fukuyama
en même temps ('at the same time') 3–4, 27, 55, 103
entrepreneur 49
  see also cult of entrepreneurship (in Macron, Emmanuel)
entrepreneurship 23, 83–86, 91–94
  see also cult of entrepreneurship (in Macron, Emmanuel)
equality 1, 63–65
European Commission 46, 102
Europe Écologie Les Verts (green party) 98, 101, 111
  see also Jadot, Yannick
European elections of 2019 8–9
European Medicines Agency 46
European Monetary System (EMS) 33–34
European Union (EU) 3, 10
  critique of 98, 111–112
  economy of 101–102
  fiscal stimulus in 55–56
  military integration of 57
  support for 99
  technocracy of 56
  withdrawal from 106
Eurozone 101–102, 106

F

Fabius, Laurent 10
face coverings 89–90
Fillon, François 6, 10, 90–91, 101
Five Star Movement 74, 76
foreign policy 55–58, 103
Foucault, Michel
  epidemics 102
  Foucauldian genealogy 13
  Foucauldian ontology 14
  techniques of power 40–48
    architecture of the town 41–42
    epidemic of smallpox 43–44
    regulation of the price of grain 42–43
    technologies of security 16, 39, 40–48, 51–52, 59
  see also security; Panopticon; Bentham, Jeremy
fourth right 24–31
Franklin, Benjamin 87
fraternity 1
French First Republic 17
French Third Republic 89
French Fifth Republic 6, 7, 8, 26, 29, 97, 109
French Sixth Republic 109–110
French interior ministry 21–22
French legislative election
  of 2017 3, 6–7, 74

INDEX

French presidential election
  of 2007 23
  of 2012 18
  of 2017 2, 6, 10–11, 13, 83
    campaign 50, 80, 99
    debate 90
    electorate 100
    results 34
  of 2022 2, 5, 6, 9, 11–12, 16, 24
    campaign 99, 105
    far right 98–99
    left 99–100
    results 96–101
French Revolution 24–26, 28, 41, 47, 53, 88–89
Frexit 11
Friedman, Milton 109
Front National party (FN) 2–3, 11, 81, 84
  antisemitism of 99
  communists and 110
  COVID-19 pandemic and 51
  logo of 49
  support in the cities for 107
Front Populaire 53
Fukuyama, Francis 6, 10

G

Gadamer, Hans-Georg 13, 14, 15
Gaullism 2, 26–27
Gaullist right 104–105
Geoghegan, Vincent 78
Germany 37, 46, 53
  army of 57
  Chancellor of 102
  deficit-financed policies of 54
  Franco-German relations 55–56
  investment in 83, 103
gilets jaunes 61, 69
  historical social movement 90, 99–100, 110
  meritocracy 104, 110
  protests of 21, 30–31, 42, 50, 58, 70, 75, 111
  public enemy 46–47
  support for 9
  tax on fuel 4–5, 8, 29, 68
  violence against 58
Giscard d'Estaing, Valéry (VGE) 8
global financial crisis of 2008 4, 19, 33, 35, 36
globalization 10, 106
grace 16, 60, 67–69, 71
  see also Calvin, John
grandes écoles 8
  see also universities
Greece 102

H

Hamon, Benoît 20, 100, 107, 109
Hansen, Lene 14

Hegel, Georg Wilhelm Friedrich 6, 15, 70
Henri IV 27, 88, 92
Hesiod 78–79
Hidalgo, Anne 97, 105, 111
history of ideas 13
Hollande, François 4, 8, 10, 12, 100, 104–105
  neoliberalism of 34
  presidency of 3, 6, 17, 19, 28, 90, 107
hope 16
  absence of 80
  as an affect 77–80
  calamity 78
  community and 86–88
  definition of 77–78
  mercy and 79
  message of 81–82
  punishment and 78–79
  solidarity and 110
  Spinoza and 79–80
  unhope 80, 82, 94
  see also ataraxia; Comte-Sponville, André; désespoir; Geoghegan, Vincent; Obama; Barack; Nietzsche, Friedrich; Révolution; solidarity; Spinoza, Baruch
Hugo, Victor 82
Hungary 103

I

ideology 15–16, 76, 100
Impôt de Solidarité sur la Fortune (ISF) (the Solidarity Tax on Wealth) 4, 28–29, 35, 62, 85
individual responsibility 65, 71, 73–74, 93
  see also Nietzsche, Friedrich; responsibility
industry 37
  financial 18, 35
  green 23
  innovation and 76
  luxury-brand 83
  pharmaceutical 46
Industrial Revolution 53
Institut d'Études Politiques de Paris 66
Institut Pasteur 37
International Monetary Fund (IMF) 35, 54
interventionism 5, 103
Iraq 84, 89
Islam 89–91, 98, 106, 107
Islamism 58, 82, 98, 106
Islamo-leftism 98
Islamophobia 11, 98
Italy 74

J

Jadot, Yannick 97–98, 111
Jews 89
John Paul II 88

Jospin, Lionel 34
July Monarchy 17, 24

K

Kerry, John 87
Keynes, John Maynard 99–100

L

La France Insoumise party (LFI) 3, 9, 97, 107, 111
la gauche caviar 100
La Grande Marche 75
laïcité 88–91
Lallement, Didier 50
La Manif pour tous (social movement) 10, 90
La Métropolitée 41–42
La République En Marche! party (LREM) 3, 6, 19, 99
  campaign of 51
  centre-left politics of 12
  establishment of 20
  European election and 8–9
  logo of 49
  political agency of 74
  structure of 4
  victory of 7, 50, 74–75
Lassalle, Jean 99
Laurence, Jonathan 91
Le Grand Débat National 75
Le Maire, Bruno 85
Le Maître, Alexandre 41–42
  see also La Métropolitée
Le Monde 14, 54, 90
Le Pen, Jean-Marie 51, 98, 99
Le Pen, Marine 2, 3, 6, 12, 50
  antisemitism of 99
  campaign of 11, 100, 105–107, 108
  Catholics and 104
  European Union and 99
  fear and 106
  neoliberalism of 99
  political program of 11, 96, 99
  populism of 81
  rhetoric against 10, 51
  rise of popularity of 82, 98–99
  secularism and 91
  support for 111
Les Républicains party (LR) 2, 6, 8, 9, 101
  death of 104–105
liberalism
  and neoliberalism 32, 34–35, 39, 105
  definition of 31–32
  fall of 36
  history of 31–32
  victory of 6–12
  see also libertarianism; neoliberalism
liberal-libertarian compromise 61–62
  see also *liberalism*
libertaire 62

liberty 1
Libya 57
Llorca, Raphaël 21, 48, 49, 50, 51
  see also neutralization
Louis XIV 27, 88
Lovejoy, Arthur 78
  see also hope
Luther, Martin 65–67
LVMH 83–85

M

Machiavelli, Niccolò 51, 52
  see also *The Prince*
Macron, Emmanuel
  analogy of the lead climber 21–24, 36, 38
  birthplace of 3
  branding of 48–49
  campaign of 100
  career of 19
  cult of entrepreneurship 21–24, 29, 66, 68, 72–76, 84, 88, 91–94
  economic reforms 28–31, 38, 62, 94, 101
  economy minister 4, 7–8, 19–20, 34
  education of 7–8, 18, 66, 74, 88–89, 111
  foreign affairs 55–58, 103
  globalist agenda of 96, 99–100
  hope and 77, 80–83, 96
  ideology 1, 6, 13–16, 17, 24, 31, 60
    and equality 62–65
    and solidarity 95
    right wing 100
  increase of social spending 30–31
  individual responsibility 73–74
  interventionism of 56–57
  legacy of 3–5
  legal reforms 19–20
  liberalism 6–12, 34–35, 39
  deregulation 19–20, 23
  meritocracy 2, 16, 31, 69–71, 99, 101, 107–109
  need for security 39, 47–48
  neoliberal reforms 4–5, 9, 12, 16, 36, 96, 104
  neoliberal ideology 17, 21–23, 28, 37–38, 39, 84, 99
  neutralization of politics 48–51
  new right 2–3, 12, 27, 96, 100, 105, 107–108
  philosophy of 3–4, 66–67
  political moderate 9–11
  political program's contradictions 4–5
  political theology 2, 16, 60, 73–74, 92
  president of the rich 28–29, 100–101
  religion 4, 88
  republican tradition 1
  social reforms 5, 20–21, 102
  security 52–53, 98, 106, 108–109
  solidarity 94–95

state security 2, 21, 39–40, 44–45, 47
technocrat 4, 7, 19, 47, 56, 69–71, 74
trickle-down economics 21–22
unemployment reforms 72–73
see also Attali Commission; austerity policies; foreign policy; hope; individual responsibility; Révolution; neutralization; new right, political theology; technocracy; trickle-down economics; unemployment; welfare
macronades 68, 71
Macron boys 70, 75
Macron law 4, 19–20
Mali 5, 56
Maréchal, Marion 99
Marx, Karl 15
Mauritiania 56
May Day demonstration 110–111
Mélenchon, Jean-Luc 3, 9, 12, 107, 111–112
  French presidential election of 2022 97–98, 101, 105, 108
merit 60, 65, 69, 71, 74, 94
  assemblage of 16
  definition of 60, 87
  promotion of 4, 31, 38, 104, 107–109
  rewarding 77
  tyranny of 70
  value of 61, 96, 101
  see also meritocrat (in Macron, Emmanuel); Sandel, Michael; universities
meritocracy 1, 2, 31, 69–71, 103, 104
  model of 68
  technopopulism and 75–76
  see also meritocrat (in Macron, Emmanuel); Sandel, Michael; technopopulism
Mill, John Stuart 31
Mitterrand, François
  critique of the French constitution 109
  liberal reforms 22, 28, 53, 64, 98
  politics of austerity 33–34
  rise of inequality 85
Modern Monetary Theory 111
Mondon, Aurélien 98, 108
Mouvement Démocrate party (MoDem) 7, 100
Muslims 89, 90–91, 106–107
  religious freedoms 5
  see also Islam, Islamism, Islamophobia
Muxel, Anne 3

N

Napoleon I 26, 27, 49, 88, 92
Napoleon III 24
Napoleonic Wars 25, 54
National Assembly 6–7, 27
  Fillon affair 91
  future of 111–112
  legal reform and 20
  reform of 8
  weakening of 50, 74
nationalist right 24, 26–27, 107
  see also Bonapartism; Orléanist right; new right; right-wing politics in France, ultra right
natural order 25
neoliberalism 84, 96, 99
  characteristics and history of 30, 31–36
  definition of 16, 32–33
  failure of 36–38, 110
  French politics and 17–18, 39
  French socialists and 105
  inevitability of 12
  negative effects of 15
  rise of 2, 13, 48, 49, 101
  state interventionism and 35–36
  see also austerity policies, liberalism, welfare
Nestlé 19
  see also Brabeck, Peter
Netherlands 46
neutralization 8, 16, 48–51, 70
  see also technocracy
New Democrats 33
New Labour 12, 33, 74, 76
new left 107–112
new right 96
  characteristics of 27, 104
  emergence of 2, 12, 16, 24
  ideology of 108
  see also Bonapartism; Orléanist right; nationalist right; right-wing politics in France, ultra right
Nietzsche, Friedrich 60, 71–74, 77, 78
  see also causa sui; hope; individual responsibility
Niger 56
Nineteen Eighty-Four 41
  see also Orwell
Nozick, Robert 60, 62–63, 92

O

Obama, Barack 23, 27, 80–82, 86–87
  see also hope
Occupied 102
open society 10, 11, 51, 55, 77, 106
  see also Popper, Karl
Operation Barkhane 56–57, 103
organicism 25
Orléanist monarchy 31
Orléanist right 24, 25–26, 27
  see also Bonapartism; nationalist right; new right; right-wing politics in France; ultra right
Orwell, George 41

P

Palombarini, Stefano 12, 19, 33, 34
Pandora 78–79

panopticon 41
  see also Bentham, Jeremy; Foucault, Michel
Parti Communiste Français (PCF) 34, 46, 97, 105, 112
Parti Socialiste (PS) 6, 7, 8, 20
  2012–2017 politics of 3
  bourgeois bloc and 29, 34
  centre-left politics 12
  death of 104–105
  European Union 10
  liberal turn and 3, 12, 64
  presidential candidate of 8, 100–101
  rule of 105
  structure 111
  support for 2, 9
  see also bourgeois bloc; Hidalgo, Anne
Paul the Apostle 79
  see also Christian theology
Pécresse, Valérie 101
Pedder, Sophie 18, 19, 39, 53, 60, 63–64, 81–82
pensions 36, 53, 92
  reforms 3, 5, 29–30, 59, 101, 108
  private 20
Perret, Gilles 111
Pfizer 19
Phelan, Sean 32, 33
Philippe, Édouard 8, 69–70
Philippe, Louis 25
physiocrats 42
Piketty, Thomas 54, 71, 85
Pius X 88
Plan Vigipirate 58
Plato 33
Poland 88, 103
political antagonisms, rise of 3, 104
political theology 2, 65, 92–93
  see also political theology (in Macron, Emmanuel)
police
  budget 102
  security measures 44–45, 90, 107
  state's body 21, 50
  violence 45–46, 48, 110–111
  see also gilet jaunes; security; state security (in Macron, Emmanuel)
Popper, Karl 10
  see also open society
Poutou, Philippe 97, 107–108
Prometheus 78–79
Protestant ethic 60, 65, 71
  see also Weber, Max
Putin, Vladimir 27, 57, 103

R

Rassemblement National party (RN) 2, 8, 11, 81, 99, 106–107
  see also Le Pen, Marie
Rawls, John 32, 60, 61–62, 63

Reagan, Ronald 22, 64, 85
recognition, principle of 70–71
Reformation 65–66
regressive taxation 4, 28–29, 71, 84, 86
  see also tax reforms
Rémond, René 24–26
Renaud (French singer) 46
reproduction technologies 5
republicanism 1
responsibility 71–74
Restauration 17, 24–25
research methods 13–15
Révolution (political program) 1, 13–14, 31, 66, 88
  charity 91–92
  equality 60
  hope 82
  job market 83
  state of the nation 18
  unemployment 72
  see also hope; Macron, Emmanuel
Rheims 25
Ricœur, Paul 14
right-wing politics in France 24–26
  see also Bonapartism; Orléanist right; nationalist right; new right; right-wing politics in France, ultra right
Rothschild Bank 18–19, 66
Rousseau, Sandrine 97
Roussel, Fabien 97
Royal, Ségolène 10
Ruffin, François 111
Rumsfeld, Donald 84
Rushdie, Salman 89
Russia 46, 55, 93, 102, 103
Russian invasion of Ukraine 27, 46, 57, 77, 103

S

same-sex marriage 10, 34, 90, 104
Sandel, Michael 22–23, 60, 69–71
  see also meritocracy
Sanders, Bernie 98
Sanofi 37
Sarkozy, Nicolas 1, 4, 19, 23, 28, 29, 58
Sartre, Jean-Paul 82
Scholz, Olaf 57
Sciences Po Paris 66, 75, 104
Second World War 48, 54
secularism 60, 65–68, 71–72, 88–91, 93–94
secularized hope 91–94
  see also charity
security 96, 108–109
  apparatus 2, 16, 42–43, 50, 70, 98, 103
  national 39–40, 47–48
  neoliberalism and 39
  see also Bentham, Jeremy; COVID-19; Foucault, Michel; Panopticon; state security (in Macron, Emmanuel)

INDEX

Simpson, Joe 22
smallpox 41, 43, 102
  see also Foucault, Michel
SNCF (French national railway company) 29
solidarity 2, 4, 80, 94–95, 101, 108
  charity and 92
  hope and 110
  model of 22
  politics and 28–30
  social 33, 53–54
  value of 110–111
Spinoza, Baruch 16, 77–80, 81–82
  see also hope
state of exception 47–48
  see also Agamben, Giorgio
sûreté 51–55, 59
  definition of 40
Sweden 56
Syria 57

T

Taubira, Christiane 97
tax reforms 4–5, 28–29, 62, 69, 85
  see also economic reforms (in Macron, Emmanuel); regressive taxation
technocracy 60, 69–71
  COVID-19 pandemic 48
  ideal of 8, 74
  notion of 47
  rise of 16, 110
  see also neutralization; technocrat (in Macron, Emmanuel)
technocratic changes 4, 7, 19, 69–70, 109–110
  see also technocrat (in Macron, Emmanuel)
technocratic politics 56, 69, 74
  see also technocrat (in Macron, Emmanuel)
technopopulism 74–76
  see also technocrat (in Macron, Emmanuel)
Thatcher, Margaret 22, 64
The Prince 52
The West Wing 61
Third Way politics 33, 49
Treaty of Lisbon 10
trickle-down economics 21, 36, 43, 84–85, 93, 99
Trump, Donald 9, 82
Turkey 102

U

Ukraine 27, 46, 57
ultra right 24–25, 27, 105–107
  see also Bonapartism; Orléanist right; nationalist right; new right; right-wing politics in France
unemployment 64–65, 72–73, 82, 83, 92
  benefits 5, 30, 101, 108
  insurance 21, 29, 36, 59, 65
United Kingdom 12, 15, 20, 31, 34, 37
  army 56

Brexit 9
defined contributions 20
government 103
neoliberalism 13
New Labour 74
public debt 54
vaccine for COVID-19 46
welfare state 53
United Nations 55
United States of America 9, 12, 23, 27, 30, 34
  administrative appointments 50
  economic stimulus 55–56
  defined contributions 20
  interventionism 103
  meritocracy 69
  neoliberalism 13
  New Deal 70
  vaccine for COVID-19 46
universal basic income (UBI) 108–109
universities 8, 103–104
  see also merit
utopia 42, 62, 69, 87–88, 92, 94
  liberal 56
  market 64
  see also Bloch, Ernst; Nozick, Robert

V

Valls, Manuel 7, 20, 34
Varoufakis, Yanis 102
Vanini, Lucilio 40
Versailles Palace 27–28
Vichy France 1, 99
von Bismarck, Otto 53

W

Warsaw Uprising of 1944 88
Weber, Max 2, 60, 65–67, 71, 87
welfare 18–24, 63–64, 108
  benefits 5
  decline of 53–54, 59, 64
  rise of 53
  state 24
  see also austerity policies, neoliberalism, Macron law
Western Africa 5, 56–57, 58, 103
Western capitalism 65–69
Winter, Aaron 98

X

Xiaoping, Deng 22

Y

Yates, Simon 22

Z

Zeckler, Michel 45
Zemmour, Éric 11, 51, 58, 82, 99–100
Zeus 78–79

www.ingramcontent.com/pod-product-compliance
Lightning Source LLC
Chambersburg PA
CBHW060031040426
42333CB00042B/2308